A Journey to Inner Joy and Peace

# A Journey to Inner Joy and Peace

*Marlene Kreidler*

Deeds Publishing | Athens

Published by Deeds Publishing in Athens, GA
www.deedspublishing.com

Printed in The United States of America

Cover design by Mark Babcock.

ISBN 978-1-950794-41-6

Books are available in quantity for promotional or premium use. For information, email info@deedspublishing.com.

First Edition, 2023

10 9 8 7 6 5 4 3 2 1

*To the memory of my courageous dad and*
*beloved mom, Otto and Rosa.*

# Contents

Foreword xi
Preface xiii
Acknowledgements xvii

1. Before the Journey 1
2. Two Girls' Journeys 9
3. Spiritual Discoveries 15
4. Wonderful Hamburg 23
5. Cargo Ships and Tugboats 29
6. Learning and "Learning" 37
7. His Journey to Inner Peace 43
8. Discovering and Finding Peace 55
9. The City of Peace 63
10. His Soft Voice 71
11. Wonders Never Done Before 79
12. At Lake Michigan 87
13. Experiencing Joy 93
14. Being Like Jesus 103
15. Resentment 109

16. I Have Called You Friends       119
17. Who are my Brothers and Sisters?       127
18. Beloved Nephews and Nieces       135
19. Kill them with Love       141
20. Amazing Grace       147
21. A Continuous Journey       151

Epilogue       157

About the Author       163

# Foreword

This book, "A Journey to Inner Joy and Peace," are the memoirs of Marlene, a collection of anecdotes that capture special family events, but in particular of our younger sister, Marlene, whom we lovingly call Kitty. We grew up together, so many of her experiences are mine too, including joys, sorrows, anger, and many surprises. People thought we were twins because when we were little, Mom almost always dressed us in twin-like clothes. And well, the difference in age and size was very small, barely 11 months and 3 weeks, for which, to this day we are both the same age for a week! The beauty is that, in a spiritual sense, we are twins, because we both decided to be born into a new life in Christ Jesus on the same day and year.

I want to thank Marlene for the effort put into compiling these experiences, which she has described with the utmost clarity, simplicity and candidness, elements that give an invaluable value to her stories.

May the reading of these memoirs not only inform the

reader about an important part of our mother's life and Marlene's spiritual journey, may they also serve as an inspiration for development and spiritual growth of the reader.

— **Elizabeth (Coqui) Kreidler de Santa Cruz**

# Preface

*"Marlene, you need to write your story,"* my friend Manny at Andrews University in Berrien Springs, Michigan, used to tell me. Somehow Manny found inspiration in my story mixed with challenges, joys, discoveries, and inner peace.

*"Mamá, write your story. Your grandchildren and great-grandchildren need to know how you met the Lord,"* I used to tell my mother as she was aging, and she couldn't make sense of her life and why she was living so long, *"You are here to pray for us, while we are busy working, we need your faith and power of prayers. It is the time for you, mamá, to write your story so we may always remember how you met the Lord."*

My mother was a woman of prayer; although she did not boast religiosity, the evidence was in her peaceful and exemplary life. She left behind a wonderful family filled with a legacy of faith and courage, but she did not write her story.

Since 2002, when my friend Manny encouraged me to write my pilgrimage to inner peace, I have written in my journals spiritual epiphanies while spending time in Bible studies and prayer. All these journals are unpublished and one day they might be destroyed. On a Sabbath in September 2021, my friend Rachel invited me to her writing club. As an English scholar and professor at Southern Adventist University in Collegedale, Tennessee, Rachel felt inspired to write about her own spiritual journey. She organized a small group that met weekly for 10 weeks and would share one chapter per week. Rachel is the encouragement I needed to organize the different life events that have led me to where I currently am, and for that I am very grateful.

Reflecting many times on my spiritual pilgrimage, and after sharing my stories with other people, sometimes I wondered if the exercise was too self-centered. Probably my two girls, Vanessa, and Valerie, would get too tired of hearing how the Lord had guided our path and blessed us. Dr. Winston Craig, Professor at Andrews University, reminded me that it was something we ought to do. He quoted from Deuteronomy the passage below, before Moses and the Israelites had entered the promised land. Repeatedly the Lord emphasized that our stories should not be forgotten, we should teach them, we should repeat them constantly, and we should write them.

> [9] *"Only be careful and watch yourselves closely so that you do not forget the things your eyes have seen or let them fade from your heart as long as you live. Teach them to your children and to their children after them.* [10] *Remember the day you stood*

*before the LORD your God at Horeb, when he said to me, "Assemble the people before me to hear my words so that they may learn to revere me as long as they live in the land and may teach them to their children."[1]*

*[19] "Teach them to your children, talking about them when you sit at home and when you walk along the road, when you lie down and when you get up. [20] Write them on the doorframes of your houses and on your gates."[2]*

To those who read my story, I encourage you to write about your own journey so that you may inspire others. After all, the Bible is full of narratives of people's individual odysseys. I hope and pray that my story brings you blessings in finding inner peace.

---

1. Deuteronomy 4:9-10
2. Deuteronomy 11:19-20

# Acknowledgements

As I meditated while writing these memoirs, my heart is full of gratitude to the many people who blessed my life. Even as an adult after my parents have been gone for so long, I still remember their teachings to have a disciplined and reflective mind. My siblings were the heroes that constantly inspired me to greatness. My nephews and nieces brought much laughter to my life. My daughters filled me with love, joy, and patience. My husband taught me to be thoughtful. My friends to be loving, my teachers to be dedicated and aspire to be a forever learner. And I learned from coworkers that life is full of challenges.

Yet this book came to fruition thanks to the inspiration of my loving friend Rachel Byrd and the writing club she began in September 2021. During the weekly meetings, hearing the stories of our group was a continuous encouragement to writing the weekly stories. Melody, Marcia, Cherie, and Ruthie, thank you so much. I owe much gratitude to the loving Cathy Lewis who initially edited my story on her own time. There were also two cheerleaders at work and at home — my boss Michael that allowed me to leave the office early every Wednesday evening, and my husband James who didn't mind me coming home late each Wednesday. Finally, my siblings Coqui, Lita, and Pepe. Coqui for her inspiration through my life; Lita, and Pepe for reading the manuscript for historical accuracy.

My heart rejoices with gratefulness.

# 1. Before the Journey — The Story of My Mother

*"Rosa te dieron por nombre, Oh Rosa de nuestro jardín,*
*Serás para nosotros siempre, Amor y ternura sin fin."[3]*

She was the daughter of a French musician who migrated to Santa Cruz, Bolivia, in the early 20th century. Gastón Guillaux composed the music for the Santa Cruz Anthem and there is a school named after him. Abuelito Gastón, as the family called him, had lost the eyesight of one eye while very young. He married Abuelita Micaela Balcázar, and had seven children—Luisa, Blanca, Pablo, Rosa, Margarita, Julio, and Carmen. In the evenings, Abuelito Gastón would ask two of his daughters, tía Blanca and my mother Rosa, to read to him. At a very young age, these ladies read newspapers, Victor Hugo, Tolstoy, and other classical writers. Rosa was a very smart and cultured lady, well versed in many topics, from ancient history to current events pub-

---

3. Acrostic to mom composed by our brother Buby in a Mothers' Day card —Rosa was the name given to you, Oh Rosa from our garden, For us you will always be, Love and tenderness without end.

lished in newspapers he received from Argentina. Abuelito Gastón was very patriotic and strong in French history, so he changed my mother's birthday to November 11, three months after her birth, commemorating Armistice Day. (Abuelito Gaston changed also tío Julio's date of birth to July 14, Bastille Day).

In 1943, mamá married very young to a handsome German galán with whom she had six children. My dad, Otto Alfonso Kreidler, was the only son of my grandfather Joseph who migrated to Bolivia in 1907. They were devout Catholics and were surrounded by two very conservative families. Dad was an active politician who, along with other intellectuals and activists in Santa Cruz, participated in a political party opposing the very first leftist and populist government of that time in South America. Because of his strong political views, dad was persecuted, imprisoned, and exiled for many years. He even was an active participant in the very first air revolt in the world when 47 political prisoners were being transferred from Santa Cruz to a concentration camp in La Paz.

In 1957, while dad was in exile, an evangelical preacher was giving studies about the prophecies and last-day events. Mom and other neighbor ladies began attending those seminars and immediately she was captivated by the historical accuracy and was impressed that they had been predicted in the Bible. Through further studies, she was baptized into the Seventh-day Adventist (SDA) Church. As the whole local society and the family were devout

Catholics, she was rejected by her beloved family who had been very supportive while our dad was a political runaway. Even worse, dad's oldest sister wrote him a letter saying to divorce that heretic and *"send me your firstborn son, José (Pepe) so that I would raise him away from that woman."* There was a wiser aunt, dad's second sister tía Norah who opened his eyes to admire the woman that supported him during his struggles, raising six young children on her own (ages 1 to 14) and did not seek the arms, money, or protection of another man.

When dad returned from exile and thoroughly discussed our mother's conversion to Adventism, mom showed him that among the 10 tenants of the political party he had joined and supported, they had written religious liberty. Mom held him accountable for his own principles. They came to an agreement that mom could go to prayer meetings on Wednesday evening and church services on Saturday morning.

One year later, in 1958 after five years of their youngest son Elmar (Chichín), my sister Elizabeth (Coqui) was born. Almost twelve months later, I was born in 1959. Mother cried because she thought six children were enough. Yet she found consolation that these two girls were the daughters of her new faith. And very surreptitiously, mom instilled in Coqui and me the love to God, the Faith in Jesus, the hope of Christ's second coming, and inner peace. Every Wednesday evening, we would walk 12 blocks to prayer meetings. Mom would arrive 30 minutes early so she and other pious ladies would pour their hearts to the Lord in prayer. Every Sabbath morning, we would make the same walk and mom would begin a smaller Bible study class at 8:00 AM, then Sabbath School at 9:30 and church service at 11:00 AM.

Mom lived an abundant life through age 84. She was rewarded with the spiritual conversion of four children and witnessed a spiritual revival among her nephews and nieces. Through the end, mother never lost her faith and first love. During her life she had been the Adventist School Principal, Church Treasurer, excellent Sabbath school teacher, and most beloved wise lady at the local church. She studied her Bible daily, analyzed passages with a Bible dictionary, comparing passages from an encyclopedia, and studying the maps. Mom read all books available from E.G White, was very faithful with her tithes, and had a heart to serve those in need.

In addition to devotedly studying daily her Bible, mom was also very faithful with her giving through her tithes and offerings.

> *"Bring the whole tithe into the storehouse, that there may be food in my house. Test me in this, says the Lord Almighty, and see if I will not throw open the floodgates of heaven and pour out so much blessing that there will not be room enough to store it."[4]*

4. Malachi 3:10

This Bible verse made a remarkable impression in my mom. Once she understood that one tenth of our earnings belongs to the Lord, she committed to honor the sacred teachings. She did not try to argue by reasoning that it was meant for the Israelites in ancient times. Mom did not question how the funds were used, neither did she make excuses that dad was in exile while being a single mother of six children. Mom obeyed what she considered a Biblical command. Every month, after receiving her wages, mom would return ten percent of her earnings to the Lord. After receiving her salary, she would separate the money into various envelopes to cover the household expenses plus her tithes. She had marked 70 Bolivian Pesos in the tithe envelope waiting until the Sabbath to take it to church.

*"Mom, mom, mom,"* the excited Chacho entered the house looking for mom until he found her as she was putting the envelopes away. *"Mom, I have a great opportunity, my cousin Tacha is taking the train to Brazil to visit his mom. We can stay there, visit the city, and then come back in two weeks. Oh, mom, this is so exciting, I want to go with him. I have never been in Brazil or traveled by train. I'm on vacation and this is the perfect time to go. The train is about to leave, I just need 70 pesos for the roundtrip ticket. Can I please go, please, please mom?"* Chacho kept pleading while mom was shuffling the money in her head ... *"if I give Chacho the 70 pesos from my tithes, I could borrow from this to do that ..."* She kept doing the math in her mind, *"mom, please don't think too much, the train is about to leave, please mom."* Mom

gave in, rationalizing that she would make up the tithes in other ways.

Pulling the tithe envelope, she handed Chacho the 70 pesos who was already packing a few belongings in a little bag. The thrilled young guy kissed mom and left to this lifetime adventure. A few weeks later, mom saw the thin, hungry, and devastated figure of Chacho entering our home. What had happened? How was his wonderful adventure? *"Mom, after we left,"* Chacho began, *"the train stopped. I got out of the train to eat something, and the train left me. I tried to catch up by jumping into a cargo train transporting vehicles. Since the cars where not locked I was able to sleep in one of them. By the time I was able to catch up with the original train, someone had come and taken my bag. Tacha and I continued the train ride to his mother's house in the city of Corumbá, Brazil. Since I had no money to purchase the return train ticket and no money for food, I had to do all sorts of odd jobs at the border by helping people carry their bags over across the frontier from one country to the other."*

Somberness fell into mom, on one hand her son was alive, hungry, beaten, and discouraged, but he was home. Why did it happen? For his trip, Chacho had taken his best few garments. A few days later, mom went to the store to purchase and replace some of the clothes that had been stolen. At the cash register she observed the total, 70 pesos, the exact same amount. Whether coincidentally or not, mom understood the message. All the Bible texts referring about tithing flowed in her mind *"the tithe belongs to the Lord."*[5]

> [30] *"A tithe of everything from the land, whether grain from the soil or fruit from the trees, belongs to the LORD; it is holy to the LORD.* [31] *Whoever would redeem any of their tithe must add a fifth of the value to it.* [32] *Every tithe of the herd and flock—every tenth animal that passes under the shepherd's rod—will be holy to the LORD.* [33] *No one may pick out the good from the bad or make any substitution. If anyone does make a substitution, both the animal and its substitute become holy and cannot be redeemed."*[6]

Mom had many other stories about tithing, how the Lord had blessed her faithfulness. Indirectly she encouraged Chichin, Coqui, and me to follow the Biblical teachings. The Lord had established the tithes to remove selfish hearts from us. Unselfish giving is to be a benefit to the giver, more than the receiver. It is better to give than to receive, for God loves the cheerful giver.

Mom's genuine devotion to the Lord was the veil that protected our family; her unconditional trust in the Lord brought showers of blessings to each of us. Much of who I am, what I know, and my desire to search, research, and study the Bible, I owe to my mom. Her story is the prelude to my journey to inner peace.

---

5. Leviticus 27: 30-33

6. Idem

Thank you mom, our most beloved Rosa.

## 2. Two Girls' Journeys — My sister and I

Coqui Kreidler, how we lovingly call my sister Elizabeth, was my closest childhood friend. Only 11 months apart, we played together, went to church together, ate and got sick together, and got dressed mostly the same. We had a wonderful Sabbath-school teacher, señora Rios (or hermana Rios), another lady who got baptized against her husband's approval. Hermana Rios had six children who later mostly became missionaries. While we were children, she was an excellent Sabbath School teacher and made the Bible stories come alive.

When Coqui and I (they called me Kitty) began elementary school, we went to the German school (Colegio Alemán or Deutsche Schule). The city of Santa Cruz was small, we could walk to school—about six blocks from home. From school, we could also walk to church—another six blocks. In those days, the school-year calendar included classes on Saturdays. My mother asked the school principal, Herr Richter, to allow us to go to church on Saturdays and be absent from school. Herr Richter who had witnessed the devastation of World War II and Nazi Germany, gladly agreed, although we had to make up for the material that had been taught that day. Coqui and I were blessed by our predecessors, our sister Lita who had graduated from Colegio Alemán with flying colors, and our older siblings were also excellent students in other schools, therefore their good family name preceded us.

Every Saturday, Coqui and I would happily get ready to go to Sabbath School and wore different clothes than those worn to school. One Saturday morning while I was in first grade, my father decided we were not going to church, rather he tightly grabbed Coqui and me by the hands and rushed us to school, cussing and cursing as we walked the solitary streets that early Sabbath morning. Coqui and I were sucking in our tears and were confused about what had caused this outrage.

When we arrived at school, our classmates were astonished to see the *"Sabbathists"*—as they would mockingly call us. We didn't have our schoolbooks with us, and we were not mentally and emotionally ready for school. Once in the classroom and sitting on my pew, *"Toc, toc,"* I heard a tap on the window next to where I sat. I looked out and it was my sister Coqui motioning me with her finger to come out. The teacher didn't say anything. *"We are going to church,"* said Coqui at the door while grabbing my right hand. *"Open the door,"* commanded the 7-year-old girl to the gatekeeper to open the big school doors. He did so without questioning us. And then, hand by hand, we silently walked to church.

When we arrived at our Sabbath school class, to our amazement and surprise, the children were kneeling and praying for us. Soon after dad rushed us to school, my mother had gone to our Sabbath School class and told her-mana Rios what had happened. This fervent lady immediately told the classmates *"We need to kneel down and pray for your friends Coqui and Kitty; they are in trouble."* Little did she know that her prayer had already been answered. From the door, two little girls were watching the little six- and seven-year-old children as they prayed. This memory is vivid, although I was only six years old.

The elementary school years were very formative in developing my faith and journey to inner peace. Dad and mom would frequently argue about religion, our siblings criticized us, cousins did not care for us, and classmates thought we were weird. My first-grade teacher would tell them not to talk to the *Sabbathist* and would exclude me from school activities and special programs. Even at that young age, the deepest desires of my heart were to marry a God-loving person of my own faith so we could have a Christian family and not have the religious turmoil we had at home.

Every Sunday dad took Coqui and me to the Catholic mass. I would arrive at the Cathedral, lay down on the pew, and go to sleep. My dad used to ask me, *"Do you also go to sleep at your mother's church?"*

"No," was my answer.

*"Then, why do you sleep at my church?"*

Although I did not respond, it was because of the liturgy and darkness of the Cathedral, the abundance of images of Christ on the cross, and other 'saints' that were not attractive. Even worse, the constantly burning candles and the incense that was burnt made it difficult to breathe (I still don't like the smell of frankincense).

On the other side, every Sabbath it was a joy to go to Sabbath School, memorize Bible verses, sing songs, and participate in church plays. Coqui and I particularly enjoyed looking at the Bible storybooks our friend and pastor's daughter brought with her. Anita Justiniano and I were very active girls in church activities, thanks to her mom Hercilia, who now was our Sabbath School teacher. During those years I developed a deep love of God and the children of the world, and truly loved singing *"Jesus loves the little children, all the children of the world, red or yellow, black, or white, all are precious in his sight, Jesus loves the children of the world."*

On certain holidays we would go to a friend's farm in the faraway countryside called "Buena Vista." Señora China de Montero attended the same SDA[7] Church and had been baptized with my mom. Her in-laws, the Trapero

---

7. SDA or Seventh-day Adventist

family, had been the first converts in Santa Cruz thanks to the efforts of a colporteur in the early 1950s. Those first faithful followers of the Lord met at a house until they built the church which we all enjoyed. At señora China's Buena Vista farm, we played with her five children Perly, Lanny, Chichico, Chinita, and Tupi. From time to time, other SDA family members would also visit, one of them was Tía Tolia[8] Jimenez de Quiroz with her children Francis, Toto, and Tania—all of us much the same age. Tía Tolia would have us sing and told us Bible stories.

Tía Tolia had a sister, tía Lía Jimenez de Quiroga, who had two sons. Tía Lía was married to a military officer, the Coronel Quiroga. Years later, tía Lia played an important role by changing the Bolivian law in ending school classes on Saturdays for the whole nation. Coronel Quiroga was the Ministro de Gobierno or Secretary of State, a government position of authority and the Lord used him for this important change.

At church, we had a lot of 'tías,' (aunties) and other friends with our own values and beliefs. It was an active church. We shared struggles and joy and rejoiced with one another. Needless to say, religion came alive to us with those loving families and friends. The days going to the Buena Vista farm and attending church were days full of joy.

Living a life of contrast, even during my childhood

---

8. Tia means auntie. We called several of mom's friends at church our "tías," as a term of respect and endearment.

years, I wanted to learn more about Jesus, follow Him, and enjoy His peace. My mother continuously repeated the verse from Proverbs 22:6 *"Train up a child in the way she should go, and when she is old she will not depart from it."* I truly believe in it, having witnessed how the pious prayers of my mother while raising us were slowly answered. I learned to rely daily and constantly on our loving Jesus.

The secret to not growing up with fear, resentment, and anger at my dad was the result of constant and fervent prayers. Instead, I learned to love our God as my true Father who is waiting for us at all times, embracing us, loving us, and saying, *"Well done my faithful girl, come into your Father's arms."*[9]

---

9. Matthew 25:23 paraphrased

# 3. Spiritual Discoveries — Life in Germany

The Lord had a great surprise for our family, especially Coqui and me. Following a political revolution in 1971 and the end of fascism in Bolivia, the military took the government, swearing-in as president General Hugo Bánzer Suarez. My dad's political party was heavily involved in the coup-d'état, and one of its great leaders became Secretary of State, Mr. Mario Gutierrez Ministro de Relaciones Exteriores (Secretary of Foreign Affairs or Secretary of State).

A few days later, my dad was sworn in as the Consul General of Bolivia in Hamburg, Germany. Although my dad was German by birth because of his German-born father, my dad had not been able to acquire German citizenship and therefore could represent Bolivia.

Soon after our arrival in Hamburg, my mother searched for a Seventh-day Adventist Church. We would take the U-Bahn (underground metro) and walked several blocks to the Grindelberg Church. They had a beautiful organ that captivated me and that I could listen to for hours. At the narthex, we were greeted and immediately introduced to a host who took it upon himself to introduce us to other Spanish-speaking members. Pretty soon there was a fantastic group of five eager Bible study ladies — Clarita Abdallah, a psychologist; Elizabeth Granada, a philologist; Nellie Campbell, a housewife; Wally Butendieck, a medical student; and mom — who would insist that Coqui (now 12 years old) and I (11) attend her class so we would learn from these smart ladies. Coqui and I missed sharing time with adolescents our own age. They had a wonderful group, yet we obeyed and followed mom.

The Bible studies were very profound. These studious and smart ladies paid special attention to the prophecies of Revelation, especially after the oil embargo of 1973. They were looking for a relationship with eschatological events. Nellie's husband was a wealthy fur merchant. When he traveled, Nellie would invite the whole group to Sabbath lunches at her house. Those lunches were a real spiritual treat. During the afternoons, 30-year-old Elizabeth would come and talk to me, while Clarita would spend time with Coqui. Elizabeth and I became close friends. She would share with me stories of her own journey and encourage me to be profound, and to seek the truth. She made me feel special in the eyes of the Lord.

In November of 1973, at the Grindelberg Church, Coqui and I requested to be baptized. They immediately assigned us Frau Hildegard Schitteck as our Bible teacher. Coqui and I absorbed those studies. In the last class, Frau Schitteck did a Bible quiz and before she ended the questions, we would already answer. I remember when she asked about John 3:16 and we recited it in German, *"Also hat Gott die Welt geliebt, daß er seinen eingeborenen Sohn gab, auf daß alle, die an ihn glauben, nicht verloren werden, sondern das ewige Leben haben"* (Luther Bible 1545). *"For God so loved the world that he gave his one and only Son, that whoever believes in him shall not perish but have eternal life"* (NIV).

Coqui and I were baptized into the Seventh-day Adventist Church on Sabbath, December 15, 1973, at a different church. We did not get baptized at the Grindelberg Church because mom was flying back to Bolivia, and she wanted to witness this special 'new life' event of the daughters of her faith. Although we were strangers in that different church, everyone was nice, and we felt very special. Frau Schitteck gave each of us a card with a Bible verse.

Coqui's verse was Psalm 37:4, 5 *"Habe Deine Lust am HERRN; der wird dir geben, was dein Herz wünschet. Befiehl dem HERRN deine Wege und hoffe auf ihn; er wird's wohl machen." (Luther Bible 1545).*

*"Delight thyself also in the Lord: and he shall give thee the desires of thine heart. Commit thy way unto the Lord; trust also in him; and he shall bring it to pass." (NIV).*

My verse was Matthew 5:8

*"Selig send, die reines Herzens sind; denn sie werden Gott schauen." (Luther Bible 1545).*

*"Blessed are the pure in heart: for they shall see God." (NIV).*

I don't know if Frau Schitteck knew what she was doing, but Matthew 5:8 has been my guiding Bible verse because I want to see God, I want to have the pure heart of Jesus that leads me to inner peace.

In January of 1974, we returned to Bolivia. Once we got established in Santa Cruz, we attended our beloved childhood church. This time, Coqui and I didn't have to go to Sunday mass with dad anymore. We were already young teenagers and had a little bit more freedom. Coqui soon got very involved in Church activities, while I was confused. We had gone back to the German School, Deutsche Schule that, thanks to tía Lia and her husband the Coronel Quiroga, no longer had classes on Sabbaths. Our classmates were into partying and involved in a very frivolous life that neither one of us were attracted to.

We still very much preferred to go to our Seventh-day Adventist (SDA) church although the majority of the members were poor and with little education. The Montero sisters had all gone to a boarding academy in Argentina, Colegio Adventista del Plata, where Anita Justiniano also attended. The Quiroz-Jimenez family had moved to the Seventh-day Adventist (SDA) school in Brazil. Mom fully prohibited me to date guys that were not from our social standing, and at the same time she did not want for me to date young guys from the German School I attended because they were not Adventists.

My confusion and frustration led me to a period of introspection, reading, reflection, and writing. At church I had a friend and we liked each other, yet he needed much spiritual guidance. He was also confused (to protect his identity, I will call him John). Since I was not allowed to see John, I began to write him letters, but those were not love letters, they were missives of spiritual encouragement and conversations about his spiritual gifts. He was a genius playing the piano and church organ, he beautifully played hymns praising the Lord. At nighttime and on weekends he would play at night clubs — *"What a waste of his musical talents,"* I thought. So, I wrote to him, but I needed to pray. I needed to study the Bible, I needed to learn more and did so by reading the same 'red' books from E.G. White that mom read.

I found plenty of wisdom in Patriarchs and Prophets. Oh, how I wish I would have those letters again and think they played a part in John's true conversion as he decided to study theology at the Brazilian university. He got married, finished college, and moved back to Santa Cruz. One day, his lonely and foreign wife needed a friend and came to sit next to my mother at the church pew (I wasn't living in Santa Cruz). This lady told my mother about the letters Kitty had written her husband John years ago when they were still single. She had read the letters and kept them; it was a big surprise for my mother as she didn't know this well-kept secret. Writing letters to John helped me in my spiritual growth and it seemed they had encouraged others as well.

After graduating from high school, Coqui went to college in Lima, Peru, in January of 1977. My lifelong friend and spiritual companion was gone. Being on my own made me more involved at our church. I had excellent friends and enjoyed the time with them. However, what I truly enjoyed was my writing gift. Besides the letters to John, I wrote poetry. Some I copied; others I wrote and had in my album of spiritual poems. Many of them I memorized and recited them at church. They led me to even deeper soul searching—how could I recite about God's glory, love, mercy, kindness, when I lived a life contrary to it? It just did not make sense, and it became a subject of more prayers and meditation.

Since I was not into partying and the superficial life of schoolmates in Santa Cruz, some family members did not understand me and told mom, *"Kitty lost her identity when she lived in Germany."* Oh, how wrong they were! I had found my true identity and was developing it even further.

Graduating from high school was a joy since I wasn't going to be in a confusing environment anymore. And now it was time to make a very important decision. Growing up I had decided I wanted to be a pastor's wife, I wanted to be a missionary. As a teenager I had discovered my love for architecture. While traveling in Europe and admiring the beautiful cathedrals, I bought little souvenir replicas and collected them. I would also make cardboard models of a perfect room and decorate them. I used to tell mom that God was an Architect. It was His profession. She would just smile.

But when the rubber met the road, being an architect and a pastor's wife didn't match. What were the other options? Nursing? No, not me. Teacher? No. Accountant? Not at all. Secretary? Don't even dream. Oh boy, what is left? I discovered there was a new profession, nutrition. Oh yeah, that sounds interesting, and it would help me understand why my mother was so concerned that we get proper nourishment.

On the other hand, I wanted to go to an SDA college—who was teaching nutrition besides Loma Linda University at not such an exorbitant price? Montemorelos University in Mexico had just created their program, so, to Mexico I headed. Going to college and feeling self-righteous, I thought I had it all figured out. Little did I know the surprises that lay ahead.

But first, before I head to Mexico and college, let me go back in the next two chapters and reflect on my memories of our time in Germany and Europe.

# 4. Wonderful Hamburg — Honoring our Parents

*"Honor your father and your mother, so that you may live long in the land the Lord your God is giving you."*[10]

Looking back, and as I reflect on the formative years living in Germany, prior to starting the college experience, I realized that the Lord had many lessons He wanted to stamp in my mind.

Life in Hamburg, Germany, was full of adventures. *"What would you like for your birthday?"* dad asked. We had arrived in Hamburg on October 12, 1971, and my birthday was just a few weeks later on November 9. Riding Chichin's bicycle in the quiet streets of Santa Cruz had been a joy prior to our relocation to Hamburg. It was time now to explore this new, yet old, city. Hamburg is surrounded by two great seas, the North Sea to the west, the Baltic Sea to the northeast, bathed by the River Elbe with the Alster River as its confluence. The Alster River forms two

---

10. Exodus 20:12

large navigable lakes, the Outer Alster (Außenalster) and the Inner Alster (Binnenalster). This means that throughout the city there are smaller rivers and canals merging to these bodies of water. "The many streams, rivers and canals are crossed by some 2,500 bridges, more than London, Amsterdam, and Venice put together."[11] What this meant for an adventurous 11-year-old girl was plenty of areas to explore.

The winters in Hamburg are very cold, there had been times that the Outer Alster froze so much that cars would drive on it. In the winter of 1971, many canals froze, including the canal across from our home on Heilwigstrasse 125. Close to home there was a smaller lake in which the neighbors gathered to ice skate. Mom bought Coqui and me ice skates and we began an exciting new experience. In the summer months, the canals and lakes were colorful with row and paddle boats which could be rented.

But riding my bicycle was not dependent on begging grownups to accompany me. To rent a paddle boat required the company of an adult, not so for exploring the city in my bicycle. Pretty soon when dad asked about a specific location, I pretty much knew about it because I had either been there or went out searching for it. One day, as I was riding my bicycle, I fell down and scratched my knees. It wasn't a bad injury, but it happened at a women's health clinic. A nurse saw me through the window that I was laying on the

---

11. Wikipedia

sidewalk and bleeding. She took me in, and several nurses came around me, cleaned the area and covered the wound. When I got back home and related the story to my parents and how special I had been treated by these loving strangers, to my surprise dad got very upset. *"You will not ride your bicycle anymore,"* was his irrational order. Quietly I went to my bedroom where the bicycle was parked and took it to my parents' bedroom –*"There, you can have it,"* was my silent rebellious response.

A few minutes later, mom came to see me, she had a concerned yet loving countenance. *"Kitty,* she said, *what you have done is very disrespectful. Your father is just concerned about you, and your attitude is not correct. Go get your bicycle from our bedroom. You may ride it again."* This incident happened over 50 years ago, why do I still remember it? Because I broke an important commandment and the Lord does never want me to forget it, *"Honor your father and your mother, so that you may live long in the land the Lord your God is giving you."[12]*

What does it mean to "Honor your father and your mother?" The dictionary defines honor as 'to hold high respect.' Hmmm, my action had been disrespectful. Let's dig deeper into the Hebrew or Greek translations.

*"Most occurrences of honor in the Old Testament are translations of some form of kabod, while in the New Testament they*

---

12. Exodus 20:12

*are derivatives of timao. These terms are generally used with reference to the honor granted fellow human beings, though in some cases they are used to describe the honor a person grants God. The root of kabod literally means heavy or weighty. The figurative meaning, however, is far more common: "to give weight to someone." To honor someone, then, is to give weight or to grant a person a position of respect and even authority in one's life."[13]*

How many more little things do we say or do to our parents that are disrespectful, therefore not acknowledging their God-giving honor? Why is honoring our parents so important that God made it a center of the Ten Commandments and it is the only commandment with a promise? *"Honor your father and your mother,"* is mentioned twice in the Old Testament and six times in the New Testament.[14] But, why? Why is God putting so much emphasis on the attitude of respect children need to have to their parents? It goes back to the story of Creation. Adam was formed by the hand of God; therefore, God was Adam's Father, his Creator. God gave Adam and Eve the virtue of being pro-creators, in other words the privilege of bringing new life in the same manner God had brought life to earth.

Through Jesus in the Garden of Eden, Adam learned

---

13. https://www.biblestudytools.com/dictionaries/bakers-evangelical-dictionary/honor.html
14. Exodus 20:12; Deuteronomy 5:16; Matthew 15:4; 19:19; Mark 7:10; 10:19; Luke 18:20; and Ephesians 6:2

stories of God's love, the fall of Lucifer in heaven and how to be on our guard from this deceiver who will be tempting us. Adam related the stories he had learned to his children, and his children to their own children. God's plan for parents was to be the vessel by whom the great stories of salvation and redemption would be told to the next generations. *"Only be careful and watch yourselves closely so that you do not forget the things your eyes have seen or let them fade from your heart as long as you live. Teach them to your children and to their children after them."*[15]

God had given Adam and Eve the honor, as parents, to be the representatives of God to their children. Which means children should acknowledge in their parents the sacred responsibility given to them, and respect them for their higher calling.

Another dimension for honoring father and mother is that as children learn to respect their parents, they are learning to respect the elderly, their future supervisors, the people in authority. Respect is a basic trait for success that is so easily forgotten. With the bicycle incident, mom wanted me to learn how important it was for me to respect my dad, even in the little things.

A few years later, I had the opportunity to travel to Paris, France, in a student exchange program. Monsieur and madame Jean Jack Lemaire was my host family, Christine was my exchange sister and Isabel was the little sister. Their

---

15. Deuteronomy 4:9

grandparents (through Madame Lemaire's side) were a loving couple. Spending time with the Lemaire's was a beautiful experience of respect among each family member. We went together on a short Seine river cruise and spent time eating accompanied by Parisian music of *La Belle Epoque*.

In 2003 Vanessa, Valerie and I visited Christine and met her children. We still communicate and share stories of our families. As I look back, what I remember the most from the Lemaires was their mutual respect.

Healthy family relationships beget healthy communities. It begins at home with children honoring their parents. They are not perfect; they try and pray to be the representatives God wants them to be. *"Honor your father and your mother,"* is the commandment God gave us as children to follow—he gave other commandments to parents too. Jesus sealed this lesson in my mind through a little accident in my bicycle when I was only 11 years old. What is your story of honoring your parents?

# 5. Cargo Ships and Tugboats — Dad's Fascination at the Hamburg's Port

*"We are what we repeatedly do. Excellence then, is not an act, it is a habit."*

## —Aristotle

Let me relate another memory of our time in Germany before resuming in the next chapter with my life in college…

Dad arrived in Germany in September of 1971 with my 19 year old brother Chacho. Neither of them spoke German, Chacho spoke some English he had learned in high school. Dad was 53 years old and arriving in Germany, his dad's fatherland, was a lifelong dream. Somehow dad and his cousin, Uncle Eugen kept correspondence, who knew of dad's and Chacho's layover at the Frankfurt airport prior to their final destination flight to Hamburg. Upon arrival and while going through immigration services, dad noted that their passports had not been stamped. This was unusual and made him very nervous. He insisted that Chacho inquire about it, but the avalanche of people precluded them going back. With his meager language skills, Chacho read *"Domestic Flights,"* followed by signs in alphabetical order — Berlin, Bremen … Hamburg, Nuremberg, etc.

Once at their gate, dad was still restless because their passports have not been stamped — later Chacho learned that at that time Germany did not require a visa for Bolivian citizens. In the meantime, there was a constant announcement, first in German, *"Herr Otto Kreidler, kommen Sie bitte an die Infotheke,"* and then it was repeated in English, *"Mr. Otto Kreidler, please come to the information desk."* This announcement at the airport was being repeated for several times to no avail.

It finally caught Chacho's attention and said to dad, *"I think they are calling us."*

*"Didn't I tell you,"* dad insisted, *"our passports should have been stamped."* They were afraid of having committed an infraction in this new land, with hectic people walking in all directions, while busy agents were trying to help passengers from all over the world — *'what can be wrong?'* they wondered.

Chacho located the counter with bold letters, *INFOR-MATION*, and then he saw an officer with an "I" on his name tag. Trembling, Chacho approached him and observed next to him a gentleman standing, he was smiling and wearing a beige coat, Italian fedora hat and an umbrella. Before Chacho was able to ask anything, he heard my dad's joyful exclamation in Spanish — *"Eugenio querido, (Eugen my dear)! You are just like the pictures you sent me, look,*

*Chacho, this is Uncle Eugen. And Eugen, this is my son Chacho, he will be translating for us. Chacho, please ask your uncle how your aunt Trudel and cousins Gudrun and Gerhard are."* In the meantime, Uncle Eugen tried to mumble something, his countenance revealed his astonishment with dad's effusivity— *"I never saw dad happier,"* recalls Chacho.

Dad grabbed his 67 years old cousin by the arm, inviting him to sit next to them. But his cousin seemed to be nailed to the floor, he did not move because there was a yellow line, and he was on the other side. Finally, a security officer that was observing the excitement and being sensitive to the situation allowed these two strangers to sit on the same side, they hugged each other while dad wiped his eyes filled with tears of joy. The encounter did not last long as Uncle Eugen needed to take a train back to Stuttgart, where he lived, plus Chacho and dad needed to take their next flight.

Arriving in Hamburg was the beginning of many adventures and marvelous years for dad. One of his favorite places to visit was the Port of Hamburg, known as Germany's "Gateway to the World," the largest one in that nation, third largest in Europe, and thirteenth largest in the world.

Anytime we had visitors, we went to visit the port and watched the arrival and departure of hundreds of cargo ships moving slowly on the waters of the majestic River Elbe. Although I was only 11 years old the first time visiting this amazing place, I was intrigued by the little tugboats pulling the large cargo boats. It was explained that tugboats are essential in the management of maritime traffic. Tugboats are minuscule in comparison to the circa 400-meter vessels, many tons heavier. When arriving at the shallower waters of a river, narrow channels, or a port, a large ship cannot maneuver accurately as when navigating in the open seas. Although a hundred times smaller, tugboats are extremely sturdy and with their powerful engine can pull the vessel behind them with a strong winch that keeps them connected. Other times tugboats push the ships to help them turnaround or straighten up.[16]

Somehow tugboats have captured my imagination ever since that first encounter. Every time we are arriving at a port on a cruise liner, or when setting sail, I observe the little tugboats being in full control of the operations. The

---

16. A tug, or more commonly a tugboat, is a secondary boat which helps in the mooring or berthing operation of a ship by either towing or pushing a vessel towards the port. A tug is a special class of boat without which mega-ships cannot get into a port. Along with the primary purpose of towing the vessel towards the harbor, tugboats can be engaged to provide essentials, such as water, air, etc., to the vessel. Tugboat eases the maneuvering operation of vessels by forcing or tugging them towards the port. Mega vessels can never be maneuvered on their own. Also, with the increased boat size, they need tugboats to carry some of their domains and tow them through narrow water channels. Tugboats have become essential for non-self-propelled barges, oil platforms, log rafts etc. These are small, rather powerful boats due to their strong structural engineering. Their propulsion system is the main reason behind their enormous strength. Some secondary functions of a tugboat, along with easing mooring operation. An average tugboat has 680-3400 horsepower engines (500-2500 kW), but boats which are larger and venture out into deep waters have engines with a power close to 27200 hp (20000 kW) and a power: tonnage ratio ranging between 2.20-4.50 for large tugs and 4.0-9.5 for harbor tugs. These are incredibly high ratios, especially considering the ratio of the cargo ships or generalships that varies between 0.35-1.20. https://www.marineinsight.com/types-of-ships/what-are-tug-boats/

same happens at airports with aircraft tugs because airplanes cannot move in reverse or because the pilot's visibility is curtailed due to the plane's height.

The tugboats make me think about the tugboats in my life. What are the little things, maybe seemingly too insignificant to even consider, yet very powerful, that are controlling me? What are my blind areas needing maneuvering by an outside force? As I watched the tugboats and ponder about my own 'tugs", what comes to my mind are habits; they could be good or could be bad. Habits are the behaviors that we perform automatically and control our lives. Through the years, and by repetition a new activity becomes an unconscious habit. Popular wisdom tells us that *"thoughts become words; words become actions; actions become habits; habits become our character; our character determines our destiny."* Therefore, it starts with the little things we say.

The Bible talks about a little part of our body, of infinitesimal size compared to the rest of us, that is very powerful.

*"Likewise, the tongue is a small part of the body, but it makes great boasts. Consider what a great forest is set on fire by a small spark. The tongue also is a fire, a world of evil among the parts of the body. It corrupts the whole body, sets the whole course of one's life on fire, and is itself set on fire by hell. All kinds of animals, birds, reptiles, and sea creatures are being tamed and have been tamed by mankind, but no human being*

*can tame the tongue. It is a restless evil, full of deadly poison.*
*With the tongue we praise our Lord and Father, and with it*
*we curse human beings who have been made in God's likeness.*
*Out of the same mouth come praise and cursing."*[17]

Hmmm, is my tongue in control of my life? Or have I been able to control my tongue? How many times a day do I use words to praise and encourage others, or to accuse and destroy those around me? How is my tongue creating new good or bad habits in my life, forming my character, and setting my destiny?

Many stories come to my mind of the little things that affect us, sometimes we know and allow it; other times we don't. There are times when we think it is best to ignore the strong forces pulling us in a direction we shouldn't go. Other times we need a strong pull to center us and bring us back on track. This means that we need to constantly make a conscientious effort to evaluate our unconscientious habits that are steering us in directions we might not want to go.

There is a little habit that has helped me throughout life while navigating uncertainty and the unknown. It is the habit of prayer. It has done wonders in my life because it can move me sideways, backward, forward, upward, downward, and to all the holy places I cannot see from where I am sitting down below. Prayer opens our minds, and with

---

17. James 3: 5-10

a gentle tug, the Lord Jesus shows us where and how to change our tract. So, for now, I will let prayer be my tug-boat using faith as my winch, after all, we all need a little tug.

# 6. Learning and "Learning" — Epiphanies During the College Years

*"For I know the plans I have for you," declares the Lord, "plans to prosper you and not to harm you, plans to give you hope and a future."[18]*

*"Aeroperu announces the departure of its flight to Lima, Peru. All passengers need to board now, please proceed to gate number 1."* The confident Marlene (no longer called Kitty) boarded an airplane from La Paz, Bolivia, to Monterrey, Mexico in August 1978, through Lima, Peru, and Mexico City. When I arrived at the Benito Juarez International Airport in Mexico City, transferring to a domestic flight to Monterrey, all the terminal commotion opened my eyes to the great changes I was now facing. At that time, I was only 18 years old, alone, no dad, mom, or siblings to look after me, no protection, I was on my own.

Bible verses began to flow in my mind, reading and repeating the Psalms after boarding the airplanes gave me

---

18. Jeremiah 29:11

peace— *"Whoever dwells in the shelter of the Most High will rest in the shadow of the Almighty."[19]* I memorized and repeated constantly, *"Keep me as the apple of your eye; hide me in the shadow of your wings."[20]* Although people saw an assured person, behind the scenes I constantly prayed and repeated various Psalms, *"God is our refuge and strength, our ever-present help in trouble."[21]*

The student life in college was beautiful. We were the first generation of nutrition graduates. Being a religious college, Montemorelos University required we took a religion course each quarter. Instead, I was allowed to take theology classes which was wonderful because I had to do Bible research. My course load was heavy, taking at times 27 credits and getting up between 2:00 and 3:00 AM to study. Yet I genuinely enjoy it. The teachers had PhDs in their area of expertise. Besides mastering their subjects, they were also very caring.

It would be unrealistic to believe that the years in Montemorelos were smooth sailing. It was during the rough storms when I experienced Jesus' closest presence. I still remember clearly one evening while praying on my knees and crying with the familiar lament, *"oh Lord, why have you abandoned me, why don't you care for my distress, why, why, why?"*

Kneeling down and resting my head on a chair evoked

---

19. Psalm 91:1
20. Psalm 17:8
21. Psalm 46:1

in me the image that I was kneeling before Jesus and my arms were resting on His lap. To my surprise, when I was finally quiet and during my prayer, I imagined seeing the face of a smiling Jesus. *"Why are you smiling, don't you care for me?"* was my retort. With gentle patience and caressing my back he said, *"Marlene, Marlene, you have been so busy studying, spending time with books and in classes that you ignored me. I have always been with you, yet you didn't experience my presence because you didn't seek me. I have been longing for this moment alone with you for a long time. Now that you are here with me, close to me, leaning on my lap, of course I smile, of course I am happy, because I have you back."*

Oh, Jesus is always with us, true to His promise and the words of Psalm 91 kept resonating in my mind. *"He is my refuge and my fortress, my God in whom I trust."*[22]

There are times I thought of stopping writing and no longer sharing my stories, because of the difficulties I faced due to my own obstinacy. Yet, it is in the *"valley of the shadow of death,"*[23] when we are molded, refined, and perfected to be ready for higher challenges ahead, and—even better, to reflect who our Creator, Redeemer, and Savior is. If the prophecy of Isaiah would have been fulfilled to the letter, *"He was led as a lamb to the slaughter,"*[24] Jesus' death would have been like the one Isaac was to experience on the stone altar when an angel of the Lord grabbed Abraham's

---

22. Psalm 91:2
23. Psalm 23:4
24. Isaiah 53:7

hand and stopped him from sacrificing his own son, but the wrong Immanuel. Yet Jesus' death was on a cross, not like the lambs that were immolated representing the true Christ. Death on a cross was slow and agonizing, representing how painful it is for us to die or let go of our sinful nature, selfish and arrogant.

Instead of living for ourselves, we no longer live our desires, but Christ lives in us, polishing our imperfections and molding us to His image. How beautiful it would be that at the end of our days we can say as Paul did, *"I have been crucified with Christ and I no longer live, but Christ lives in me. The life I now live in the body, I live by faith in the Son of God, who loved me and gave himself for me."*[25]

*"Trials and obstacles are the Lord's chosen methods of discipline and His appointed conditions of success."*[26] *"The fact that we are called upon to endure trials shows that the Lord Jesus sees in us something precious which He desires to develop. If He saw in us nothing whereby He might glorify His name, He would not spend time in refining us. He does not cast worthless stones into His furnace. It is valuable ore that He refines."*[27]

It was by praying and reading books like The Ministry of Healing and its excerpt Help on Daily Living, that I learned not to trust in myself but to depend on my Goldsmith. He was refining my character and revealing my im-

---

25. Galatian 2:20

26. E.G. White, *"Help on Daily Living,"* page 8, 1964, Copyright 2010. https://m.egwwritings.org/en/book/37.23#27

27. Idem, page 9.

perfections. How nice would it be to say that when I graduated from Montemorelos University in 1980, not only did I earn a degree in Nutrition, and I also earned a degree in an impeccable character. I went to college to learn about science, yet the most precious and unexpected learning was getting to know myself and areas needing constant development.

The graduation ceremony at college is called commencement, the beginning of our professional journey. It was also a commencement to a deeper reconnaissance of my inner spiritual need. To college I went to learn, and at college I learned what I wasn't expecting to learn.

Since Montemorelos University only offered an Associate's Degree in Nutrition, the journey continued, enrolling in summer classes at Loma Linda University on La Sierra Campus in the vicinity of Riverside, California. My appetite for studying had barely touched my lips, with the intense desire to continue my career all the way until completing a PhD in Nutrition. After finishing three summer classes, the sojourn had an abrupt and unexpected denouement. Prior to the beginning of fall semester at La Sierra, I was enjoying the short break at a friends' house in Calimesa, California. The phone rang, Mrs. Westermeyer answered and said, *"Marlene, this phone call is for you."* On the other line I heard, *"Marlene, your dad and brother are at my house here is Riverside, California. I will be driving them to Calimesa, then all of you can return to my house."*

My dad had traveled to take me back home to Santa Cruz, Bolivia. There was no pleading with him that would help him reason and allow me to stay at La Sierra College to complete my much-desired bachelor's degree in nutrition. A few days later we took an airplane back to Santa Cruz. A time of uncertainty began.

Hmm, *"que será, será? Whatever will be, will be, the future is not ours to see. Que será, será, what will be will be."*

# 7. His Journey to Inner Peace — The Story of My Dad

*"You will keep in perfect peace those whose minds are steadfast, because they trust in you."[28]*

*"You will be called Otto."* Josef raised his gorgeous bundle in a warm, humid, and sunny day on Monday, November 26, 1917. I can only imagine the fuss that went around their house, when abuelita Lindaura began her labor pains, and a baby boy was born surrounded by four older sisters—Guillermina, Norah, Blanca, and Regina. Josef Kreidler, or abuelito José, cuddled his precious boy in his arms and named him in honor of his youngest brother living in Germany.

Growing up, dad was energetic, adventurous, idealistic, smart, hard-working, and very handsome. Otto Alfonso Kreidler, was the son of a German immigrant who inherited the Teutonic spirit of discipline, order, determination, and persistency. Born on June 4, 1880, abuelito José mi-

---

28. Isaiah 26:3

grated to Bolivia from Southern Germany in 1907, through a long journey via Buenos Aires, Argentina, and Paraguay. He settled in Santa Cruz, Bolivia and later built a very large house in San Ignacio de Velasco, a small Jesuit farming community in the State of Santa Cruz, east of its capital city bearing the same name.

Abuelito José also bought a large hacienda or estancia called Reyes (Kings) in which he raised cattle. He married a Spanish-descendant beau, Lindaura Rivero with whom they had a total of six children. They also had a couple of boys that were named Josef but died in their infancy. At the Reyes hacienda and in their home in San Ignacio, they had many laborers, where the girls enjoyed a life of luxury as members of the high society. Their lace dresses were imported from Germany and Abuelito José ensured they had an excellent education. Abuelito was a prominent businessman and was actively involved in the city council, being president of the local social club (Club Social) for two terms.

*"Señora, can you feed a group of 24 people?"* Asked Coqui the hostess at the Club Social's restaurant. *"What is on your lunch menu today? And can you prepare a meal for some vegetarian guests?"* Coqui was planning the noon meal for the family visiting the town of San Ignacio where our father grew up. We were celebrating his centennial on Monday, November 27, 2017. Such a large, unexpected group of tourists traveling by bus raised the attention of the local residents. While Coqui was planning the noon meal, the

administrator of the club came and introduced himself. The typical string of questions followed *"Who are you, what is your name, what brings you here, etc., etc."*

*"Oh, Kreidler, yes, I used to work with your brother Buby. He was a great person. Your grandfather, did you know he was the second president of this club? Come, let me show you."*

Somehow Coqui finished planning the meal with the hostess/waitress and the administrator's wife who got quickly to work leading the cooks in the kitchen. In the meantime, the administrator walked us through a long brick patio, unlocked the double wooden door to a large, dim, and musty ballroom. After opening a few old wooden double-paned windows, the administrator led us to a stucco wall of fame. There he was, the picture of Josef Kreidler, President of the Social Club. We were astonished! This was something we did not know. We were looking for the first time at this picture of our handsome grandfather.

Abuelito loved the family he left behind in Germany. Although he made the trip to South America looking for better opportunities, he missed his parents and siblings living at their Heidenhoff farm near Heidelberg in Southern Germany. There were nine siblings of which Josef was number five. Abuelito was very faithful and wrote loving letters to his family who were living the terror of "The Great War" (later known as World War I). His youngest brother Otto had gone to war, his loving mother had passed, and these events truncated abuelito's desire to take his older daughters to visit the family in Germany.

The missives abuelito wrote were carefully saved by his German relatives, having survived two world wars. A great contrast with the Bolivian family who burned all the letters abuelito received, personal documents, and even his German passport after his passing at a young age of 39, February 29, 1920. Years later, the loyal German family gave dad the letters abuelito José had written in beautiful cursive old German. *"I will help you understand the letters,"* Tante Ingrid said, Uncle Otto's daughter who was visiting us in Santa Cruz. Tante Ingrid read the letters to me while I wrote them in current modern German and translated them into Spanish.

Through those letters I was able to observe the soul of abuelito José, a loving son, caring father, and community leader. Not only would he send money to his family, in 1917 he also sent 50 Deutsche Mark for the German World War I efforts through the German Consul in Santa Cruz (the equivalent in 2021 of €50,000; or US $57,851). The donation record at the consular office was the only surviving document proving his German citizenship with which our family was able to later claim our own German citizenship.

Abuelito José would also save gold coins plus Silver Sterling in a wooden trunk with a special lock for dad's education. Dad enjoyed his father's affection for two years. Grandpa died and left behind a two-year old orphan and an even younger one-year old little girl, tía Frida. When dad was 15 years old, his mother passed, and from then he was on his own. Although Reyes was a very prosperous hacienda, distant relatives squandered the money, sold the estancia, their home in San Ignacio and misappropriated dad's educational funds. They mistreated and beat him like a peon.

By the age 15, he had enough and left the town penniless, never to return or make it his residence again. Dad worked very hard and put himself through a correspondence accounting school in Argentina. The hardships of life made him bitter and resentful, yet he had a profound love for the family in Germany with whom he kept contact through a first cousin, Onkle Eugen.

Once leaving San Ignacio, dad met the love of his life in Santa Cruz and was smitten by the 16-year-old smart and pretty French-Bolivian young lady, Rosa Guillaux. They soon got married and had six children, Carmen (Pimpi), Lita, José (Pepe), Alfonso (Buby), Walter (Chacho), and Elmar (Chichin). During his spare time, dad was very active in political activities. The State of Santa Cruz was required to send all their taxes to the central government in La Paz but did not get any government funding in return for their economic growth.

The State of Santa Cruz was very prosperous with agriculture (cotton and sugar cane) raising cattle, plus huge oil, and gas reserves. Yet Santa Cruz had no basic infrastructure, roads were not paved, there was no potable water, no sewage system, no electricity, and no interstate highways. It took the blood of several valorous Crucenians (demonym for people of Santa Cruz) to get back 11% of the oil and

natural gas royalties as stated in the Constitution, a fight
for their rights that began in 1957. Yet the abuses from the
central government in the city of La Paz were many. They
committed atrocities, invading the city of Santa Cruz with
troops and killing civilians, including mothers and children, just because of the rightful requests from the Crucenians.

During these turbulent political and economic times,
dad and a group of intellectuals met regularly, reviving,
and strengthening a political party opposing the fascist
government. Established in 1937, Falange Socialista Bo-
liviana (FSB) and in the 1950s they had many followers.
The response from the central government in La Paz was
an invasion of Santa Cruz, arresting anyone with the FSB
political affiliation, sending them to prison, beating them
to death after excruciating dismemberment, while alive, in
front of their families.

Santa Cruz was painted in red with the blood of their
martyrs. All around, homes had been ransacked, children
gotten up from bed screaming, their mattresses cut with
knives while the ransackers searched for any written documents or hidden citizens. There are many stories about
the atrocities of the 1950s perpetrated in Santa Cruz by
the central government led by the Movimiento Nationalis-
ta Revolucionario (MNR) under two bloody Presidents of
the decade, Victor Paz Estensoro and Hernan Siles Suazo.

During 13 years while the Crucenians struggled, the
world closed its eyes to the abominable reality facing the

State and the city of Santa Cruz. It culminated on September 25, 1956, when 47 political leaders (among them my father) were arrested from their homes and imprisoned. Through a messenger they learned they were being flown to a concentration camp in La Paz to be annihilated. All 47 of them were in a small local jail cell without mattresses, or latrines. All of them were standing and crowded for over 24 hours, which gave them time to plot their only chance for survival. In the meantime, a brave lady was able to send a revolver among food for the prisoners with a little handwritten note about their destiny.

At 5:00 AM on Wednesday, September 26, 1956, all 47 men were taken to the Aeropuerto El Trompillo in Santa Cruz and pushed to board a small four-engine plane, DC-4 with initials CP-160 from Lloyd Aereo Boliviano (Bolivian Airlines) whose engine was already running. Besides the pilot, copilot, and stewardess, the plane boarded six agents from a paramilitary group "Control Politico," (the Bolivian equivalent of the Gestapo). The six agents had large machine guns for the two-hour flight to the Panagra Airport near the city of La Paz where a large contingent of paramilitary agents awaited to take them to one of their concentration camps.

Once the plane reached proper altitude, the group of 47 prisoners, upon a signal, took control of the armed men, the armament, and plane. Among them was Saul Pinto, a well-known pilot, he took control and requested the pilot to fly them to Argentina. They landed at an airport in the city of Salta where the military and people received them with praises, food, and immediately gave them political asylum. The news traveled worldwide since this became the first aerial hijacking in world history, but only for the purpose of setting themselves free and not for any kind of ransom payment nor threatening anybody.

Several newspaper stories and books have been written about those 13 years of terror that culminated with the takeover of an airplane without the loss of one life—the 47 men had mercy of their enemies and sparred their lives. One of the books written about these historical years was authored by my dad in 1968, "13 Años de Resistencia." In 2020, a young group of Crucenian cinematographers began filming a movie called "El Salto a Salta"—The Jump to Salta. You may find more information on their Facebook page. The MNR populist government lasted through 1964 and was followed by a series of military governments.

It wasn't until 1971 when change finally came to Santa Cruz after a military coup d'état in which General Hugo Bánzer Suarez became Bolivian President. It was the end of political turmoil, bringing stability and rest, not just for our family, but for the State and city of Santa Cruz. Due to his political acumen and professional background, dad was appointed as the Consul General of Bolivia in Hamburg, Germany, where we lived peaceful and joyous years. Yet, I could always perceive a sense of resentment and sadness in my dad. Somehow his soul was wounded, and his scars could only be healed through the power of Christ and the Holy Spirit.

Dad loved to read and write; he authored and published another book that were tales of his childhood. He kept dreaming of the family and home that had been taken away from him at a very young age. He had fathered nine children, all of them were healthy, professionals, and ethical citizens. Dad had 25 wonderful grandchildren that frequently visited him. He still had a faithful and hardworking wife. He read his Bible, and prayed, yet dad still lived in sadness.

In 1993, dad was diagnosed with terminal cancer that had metastasized to his abdomen and liver. Mom and two siblings took dad to Santiago, Chile, to seek advanced medical treatment. Instead of finding hope and a cure he was given—what he called, '*his death sentence.*'

"*I want to be alone with you and pray, Rosa,*" dad said to mom back at the hotel. The two of them spent precious moments alone at their room where dad prayed and asked my mom to forgive him. At that moment he gave his life, his soul, his mind, trust, family, and hope to Christ, his Redeemer. Since his youth, dad fought for social justice, being the voice of the little ones, seeking to fill the void he lost when abuelito died. At this time, dad relented everything to Jesus.

His last few weeks were full of serenity until he exhaled his last breath on May 15, 1993, surrounded by all his children—which had always been his request. His peacefulness was evident of a soul healed by the hand of His Savior. Those precious last moments with dad brought consolation to my heart and the assurance that I will see him again. He was saved.

After the funeral, I debated with God and complained to Him. *"Why, Lord, if dad was going to be saved anyway, why didn't you, God, give us (mom, Coqui, and me) the joy of his company at church? Why was the happiness of having a Christian home with dad taken away from us? Why didn't we enjoy a loving Christian dad while he was alive?"*

Why, why, why, were my constant complaints in prayers. Until I heard God's firm and yet gentle reprimand, *"Marlene, Marlene, how selfish are you. Why are you concentrating on what you didn't have and instead concentrate on what you do have? Your dad is saved, you will see him again — why does this earthly life matter so much to you? I have eternal life for you, and a life with your dad — isn't that what you were praying for all your life? Weren't you praying for his salvation?"*

God's message shook me up, I realized how selfish my prayers had been and I was ashamed. This epiphany was a new discovery to inner peace. It was a revelation that dad was searching for *his* inner peace. He worked hard, he traveled, he engaged in political activities, and fought for social justice, trying to fill the void grandpa left. In his prayer with my mother, dad gave his life to his true Father, *"The everlasting Father, Prince of Peace, The mighty God."*[29] Dad found the answer in Jesus' words, *"I am the way and the truth and the life. No one comes to the Father except through me."*[30]

29. Isaiah 9:6
30. John 14:6

At the end of his life, dad found his inner peace with his Savior and true Father, always repeating Jesus' words he learned at church, *"Peace I leave with you; my peace I give you. I do not give to you as the world gives. Do not let your hearts be troubled and do not be afraid."[31]* My dad rests in peace.

---

31. John 14:27

# 8. Discovering and Finding Peace

*"When you make peace with yourself,*
*you make peace with the world."*[32]

How do we find peace? What is peace? I always wonder what the meaning of peace is.

*"People need to be respectful,"* an employee complained to me several times. On the opposite side I received phone calls with the same type of accusation about the complaining employee. Who was right? What was the real problem? Ah, it had to do with the definition of the word, in this case "respect."

Words have different meanings to people. An old friend used to say, *"I don't need to go to church. I don't harm anyone, I am OK."* His definition of inner peace was being and doing 'always good,' and don't worry about the rest. Other people believe that blowing up a city will lead them to a peaceful paradise. Governments have to resort to peace treaties to end hostilities that cause war with other nations. Alfred Nobel on his will wrote as a qualifier for the Nobel Peace

---

32. Maha Ghosananda

Prize as *"the person who shall have done the most or the best work for fraternity between nations."*

How did Jesus define peace? During his short three years of ministry, Jesus experienced anything but peace. He was constantly bullied, harassed, mocked, challenged, criticized, ridiculed, and finally put to death. Yet, Jesus said to His disciples at the last meal they had together, *"Peace I leave with you; my peace I give you. I do not give to you as the world gives. Do not let your hearts be troubled and do not be afraid."*[33]

What is the peace Jesus was referring to when He said the words— *My peace I leave you*? In the midst of all His ordeals, He had peace. Jesus would seek and find the source of His peace very early in the morning when He would get up and pray. Mark tells us, *"Very early in the morning, while it was still dark, Jesus got up, left the house, and went off to a solitary place, where he prayed."*[34]

Like a deer panting for streams of water, He was yearning and seeking the presence of His Father. His soul was thirsty for God, for the living God. Jesus didn't ask, *"Where can I meet with God?"* He met God, His Father wherever He was very early in the morning. It was a matter of a private and solitary place, and a matter of time.

When Jesus said, *"Peace I leave with you,"* was He referring to the absence of fear, troubles, or afflictions? On

---

33 John 14:27
34 Mark 1:35

the contrary, Jesus was not promising a life without problems. He was reassuring us *His* continuous presence with us through the Holy Spirit. Jesus found *His* peace in the continual communication with His Father who bathed Him with His presence, and Jesus wanted us to have the same source of peace—not as the world gives it to us, rather the peace that only He and His Father can bestow.

The disciples, children, and many followers loved to be around Jesus. His presence was a balm to their anxious souls. In Jesus' presence they felt the love and acceptance they had not felt before. Knowing the disciples heart, which is a reflection of our own heart, and the need we would have of Him, Jesus prayed to His Father, *"Father, I want those you have given me to be with me where I am, and to see my glory, the glory you have given me because you loved me before the creation of the world."*[35]

Oh, Jesus was praying not only for His presence, but He also wanted us to see *His* glory. And what is His glory? When Moses asked God to see *His* glory, what God revealed to Moses was the *goodness* of the Lord. In Exodus 33 we read:

*33: 18 Then Moses said, "Now show me your glory."*

*33: 19 And the Lord said, "I will cause all my goodness to pass*

---

35 John 17:24

*in front of you, and I will proclaim my name, the Lord, in your presence.*

*34: 5 Then the Lord came down in the cloud and stood there with him and proclaimed his name, the Lord.*

*34:6 And he passed in front of Moses, proclaiming, "The Lord, the Lord, the compassionate and gracious God, slow to anger, abounding in love and faithfulness,*

*34:7 maintaining love to thousands, and forgiving wickedness, rebellion, and sin."*

In other words, the goodness of the Lord or His glory is God's character—compassionate and gracious, slow to anger, abounding in love and faithfulness, maintaining love to thousands, and forgiving wickedness. Jesus was praying to His heavenly Father that we also have the same spirit. His loving character would be the source of our peace. And, with the sources of Jesus peace and His presence, our hearts cannot be troubled.

Even though Jesus offered us His peace and He prayed to the Father for his constant presence, how we can achieve it? In Isaiah we read, *"You will keep in perfect peace those whose minds are steadfast, because they trust in you."*[36]

*"… whose mind is steadfast…"* What is a steadfast mind?

---

36. Isaiah 26:3

The Spanish word used in the verse is "persevere." In other words, *"God will keep in perfect peace those whose thoughts persevere in Him."* Hmm, I needed to learn more.

Writer and blogger Terry Enns has a good analysis of Isaiah 26:3.

*First, the word "mind" is not the typical word for mind. Rather, it is a word that comes from the artist's world. It refers to a work of a potter—it is something shaped and formed by his hands. So, in a figurative sense, it refers not just to one's thoughts, but of the inclination and striving and desires of an individual. It is the shape of his mind—his purposes and plans for the way he will live life.*

*Secondly, the word "steadfast" means "to support" or "to lean"—to place one's weight on another. But the word here is a passive form, which means that the individual's mind is supported by another. He is made firm by another. The directions and purposes of his life are kept and shaped and molded by God Himself.*

*So, to be "steadfast of mind" means more than just being careful with our thoughts (though it also includes that). It means the motives, inclinations, and desires of our hearts shaped and formed by God Himself.*[37]

When we talk about a steadfast leader, we think of a

---

37. Enns, Terry, *A Steadfast Minds.* October 27, 2011. https://wordsofgrace.
blog/2011/10/27/a-steadfast-mind/#:~:text=So%20to%20be%20E2%80%9C-
steadfast%20of,Him%20(10%3A20).

dependable, reliable, consistent, unwavering, and resolute person. Oh, now I can understand Isaiah better when he says that God will keep in perfect peace the person whose mind is steadfast. It means that God will give me peace while I am persevering in anchoring my thoughts and trust in God who is the only dependable, reliable, consistent, and unwavering leader. Perfect peace doesn't come from something that I do, it comes from whom I lean on.

Slowly I began to understand what brought peace to my life was Jesus' constant presence. His companionship is possible only if I trust Him, and if I allow Him to be with me and answer to His call while He is knocking at my door and calling me by my Name. *"Here I am! I stand at the door and knock. If anyone hears my voice and opens the door, I will come in and eat with that person, and they with me."*[38]

By enjoying Jesus' presence, I can also experience the goodness of the Lord, in other words I am the beneficiary of His compassionate heart, gracious character, abundant love, amazing faithfulness, and unquestionable forgiveness. It is Jesus' presence in my life that brings me peace, regardless of the place where I am or the circumstances I face. Jesus didn't say I will be with you in the good times, He said *"I will be with you always."*[39]

Jesus also promised, *"When you pass through the waters, **I will be with you;** and when you pass through the rivers, they*

---

38. Revelation 3:20
39. Matthew 28:20

*will not sweep over you. When you walk through the fire, you will not be burned; the flames will not set you ablaze."[40]*

Jesus reassured, *"In the world you will have affliction, but be of good heart, I have conquered the world."[41]*

It was not necessary to listen to my instincts to fly and run away from circumstances; or to fight and defend my rights like my dad did and, the tenacious spirit I inherited. What I needed was learning to spend time with my Savior even in the midst of the fires or floods of life. At the same time, I decided not to engage in activities that would disturb my spirit; rather, to seek and keep activities, places, and people that would set the stage to fill my soul with peace. This is a constant and prayerful search.

---

40. Isaiah 43:2
41. John 16:33

# 9. The City of Peace — Or the Person of Peace

*"For I am convinced that neither death nor life, neither angels nor demons, neither the present nor the future, nor any powers, neither height nor depth, nor anything else in all creation, will be able to separate us from the love of God that is in Christ Jesus our Lord."*[42]

*"Kitty, Kitticita,"*—a cousin once said, *"entre Santa Cruz y La Paz, vives buscando la paz,"* –between Santa Cruz and La Paz (the city of peace), you are searching for your own peace. It was 1981, I had been living in Santa Cruz like a ship tossed by the winds that had lost its north, cast away without a course.

After my abrupt departure from Loma Linda University to Santa Cruz the summer of 1981, and determined to return to college in the U.S., I applied to Andrews University in Berrien Springs, Michigan, and was accepted. To obtain the student visa, I flew to the city of La Paz where

---

42. Romans 8: 38-39 NIV

the American Consular office was located, and my sister
Lita, her husband Adolfo, and three children lived. With
the tender motherly love that Lita had always conveyed,
she advised me to stay home, not to leave the family behind
and move so far away. She introduced me to a physician,
Dr. del Castillo, who had received a grant from Johns Hop-
kins University for a research study on the Bolivian children's growth charts. Dr. del Castillo hired me for the temporary project to visit the Indian communities in the city of
El Alto, interview infant mothers, measure their children
and begin the data gathering process. Once this task was
completed I found a job with ADRA International[43], called
OFASA[44] at that time.

Living with Lita and her family in La Paz was a joy.
It stemmed from being a single 21-year-old aunt of three
active boys who we tenderly called Adolfito, Ernestito, and
Alejandrito, ages 10 and 9 (the youngest two were twins).
Prior to finding a full-time job and on weekends, the boys
and I would play all sorts of games. Adolfito[45] liked to ex-
periment and one day gave me a bottle of his homemade
parfum—although it smelled awful, I accepted and had
to use his loving gift. Alejandro liked learning how to do
tricks, and Ernesto was quietly involved in a lot of mischief.

We would also climb the hills behind their house, walk

---

43. Adventist Development and Relief Agency, an international development
organization.
44. OFASA, Obra Filantrópica de Asistencia Social Adventista.
45. I used Adolfito for my nephew's name to differentiate him from his father
Adolfo.

through narrow and deep passages as I encouraged them with valor and tenacity. Looking down the steep cliffs, Alejandro's face depicted fear. Some Sundays, their father gave me money to take them to the movies. To their great amusement, we watched *Star Wars*—oh how much they enjoyed it! On our return home we would speed in their red Honda Prelude in the cobbled, precarious, winding, and dangerous streets of La Paz chasing good looking boys while I flirted from the car with the handsome drivers trying to pass me. The boys would stand up from their seats to see better, no seatbelts protected them. With their excited voices they encouraged me in the dangerous adventure— *"keep going, tía, faster, faster..."* is what they continually said.

In the meantime, Lita worked full-time. In the evenings, even though she looked very tired after a long day at work, she helped the boys with their homework. On weekends, Lita embroidered, baked, or cooked delicious meals. On Saturdays, I would go to church, accompanied many times by Adolfito.

The altitude of La Paz is 11,942 feet above sea level and is surrounded by beautiful mountains from the Andes mountain chain that are crowned with eternal snow peaks. The climate in La Paz is cool and mostly cloudy. Over the course of the year, the temperature typically varies from 28°F to 60°F and is rarely below 23°F or above 65°F. This means that evenings and nights are usually very cold. Homes generally don't have a calefaction system, making sleeping uncomfortable by laying underneath several layers of blankets while breathing the cold air. Yet the boys rooms were heated with their energy, and their beds were warmed with electric blankets.

Before going to sleep I would tell them stories, followed by the familiar begging, *"tía, please stay and sleep with me."* It was a difficult decision as I loved each one of them, but the charming and smart Adolfito was ahead of the game. Before I began telling the bedtimes stories in the twins' bedroom, Adolfito would start warming up his bed and played soft calming music in his room. Needless to say, his invitation for a cozy night sleep was generally accepted. Next door though, the twins began their wrestling games until exhaustion made them sleep. Other evenings, I spent time talking to Lita before her husband came home from work.

The city of La Paz means The Peace, called after Our Lady of Peace (Nuestra Señora de La Paz), another name given by Catholics to the Virgin Mary. I don't know if it was the city, or the friendship that began with my loving sister Lita that brought peace to my life. One day I said to her, *"Lita, I am a very happy person. I am happy because I live at a nice home and don't even have to pay for it. I am happy because I enjoy a family and don't even have to worry about a husband. And finally, I am happy because I don't have to deal with our strict dad."* Lita swallowed a laugh, and just gently smiled.

Through the years our friendship has grown, I look back at the years this loving sister became the caretaker of Coqui and I while she was in high school in the afternoons while mom worked, and we grew from infants to children. She strived to teach us good habits and inculcate discipline. Nowadays, we talk almost daily on the phone and could converse for hours — about books we read, food we cook, crafts we make, movies that we recommend watching, our families, our friends, our cars, pets brought to our homes, work, coworkers, and the topics are just endless.

My loving and perfectionist sister taught me how to be an adult, how to take care of myself, style my hair, take care of my money by splitting my monthly salary in envelopes to ensure all responsibilities were covered. Always the utmost professional, through her silent example I assimilated manners to be a respected and admired woman in the workplace by being organized, well prepared, always studying and continuing our professional development while swimming among the men's world full of sharks and envious females prying for the positions we earned due to our efforts and sacrifice.

When it was time to leave Lita's affectionate and comforting home, there was an inner fear of facing the unknown, after marrying Hugo and moving from La Paz to Denver, Colorado, where he lived and went to college. Denver had been Hugo's home for several years and where close relatives lived. On the other hand, it was a new place for me, everyone would be new people. There was uncertainty where I would be working, nobody to recommend me or introduce me to managers.

Who was I? I reflected that all around the world supervisors, managers, and executives depend on letters of recommendations for newcomers and people they have never met before. I kept wondering, *"Who will introduce me? Who will provide me with letters of recommendations?"* Knowing my thoughts and worries, my always loyal and loving heavenly Father had words of encouragement for me in His Word, *"Marlene, don't worry about letters or recommendations, "Do you need, like some people, letters of recommendation to you or from you? ² You yourself are the letter, written on your heart, known, and read by everyone. ³ You show that you are a letter from Christ, the result of His work in your life, written not with ink but with the Spirit of the living God, not on tablets of stone but on tablets of human hearts. ⁴ Therefore, you should have confidence through Christ before God. ⁵ Not that you are competent in yourself to claim anything for yourself, but your competence comes from God. ⁶ He has made you competent to share His love wherever you are — not of the letter but of the Spirit; for the letter kills, but the Spirit gives life."*[46]

It is just me, a person of integrity, the open letter I need to present to all the strangers I was about to meet. The personal testimony and reflection that Christ was living in me, not a farse that soon will be unveiled, but a trustworthy and ethical individual. The Lord had further advice through His Word, *¹⁶ "I am sending you out like sheep among wolves. Therefore, be as shrewd as snakes and as innocent as doves. ¹⁷ Be*

---

46. 2 Corinthians 3: 1-6 NIV, paraphrased.

*on your guard; … [18] … you will be brought before governors and kings as witnesses to them and to people that don't know me. [19] But when you are questioned or accused, do not worry about what to say or how to say it. At that time, you will be given what to say, [20] for it will not be you speaking, but the Spirit of your Father speaking through you."[47]*

Although Jesus used these recommendations to His disciples when He gave them the authority to work, the timing of the message assured me that—as long as I was Jesus' faithful servant, He was going to send His Holy Spirit as my intercessor, as I was to represent Him as an ambassador, [20] *"We are therefore Christ's ambassadors."[48]* Oh, Jesus was talking in familiar language, while living in Germany the ambassadors and consuls needed to be citizens of impeccable character representing their nations. In my case, wherever the Lord led me, I was to be His ambassador—enough said, it gave me the confidence needed to walk as the daughter of the highest King.

Yet the Lord had a few more messages. Those gems I discovered by reading the book *The Ministry of Healing.* *"Let those who work for the higher classes bear themselves with true dignity, remembering that angels are their companions.[49] So today while the humble worker for God is following her employment, angels of God stand by her side, listening to her*

---

47. Matthew 10: 16-20 NIV, paraphrased.
48. 2 Corinthians 5:20
49. E. G. White, Ministry of Healing, p. 218, Copyright 2010 by the Ellen G. White Estate, Inc.

*words, noting the manner in which her work is done, to see if larger responsibilities may be entrusted to her hands."[50]*

The Lord had been preparing me to face unfamiliar people and places. His counsel has been sealed in my mind since that early age—The Lord goes ahead of me, opens, or closes doors, while the Holy Spirit is talking on my behalf. In the meantime, angels are watching my actions and whisper in strangers' ears to trust in me and allow me opportunities of greater responsibilities.

Simultaneously with the Lord's teachings, Lita's wise counsel and patient guidance gave me the confidence to move forward in this life. Once I left La Paz, the city of peace, and lived with a woman that brought peace to my life, I wondered *"is it more important living in the city of peace or with a person of peace?"* Well, we all have a different answer. What I discovered is that the place is not a specific geographical location, it is what we make of our current circumstances, turning our environment into a place of peace, and becoming the person of peace to those around us. Just like my sister when she provided the peace to me at a most needed time.

Is it the place? Not really. Is it the person? Yes, it is. My sweet sister Lita is a true lady of peace.

---

50. Id, p. 480

# 10. His Soft Voice — Promises and Just $30 in my Pocket

*"I took you from the ends of the earth. From its farthest corners I called you. I said, 'You are my servant.' I have chosen you and have not rejected you."* [51]

Tossing in bed during a cold Wednesday night in Denver, Colorado, on November 25, 1998, I finally decided to get up and read. *"Oh, but it is only 4:00 AM,"* I thought. It wasn't insomnia, nor sickness or discomfort, it was His soft voice calling me to wake up and spend time with Him.

*"Where are we, what were we doing in this place away from our home in Santa Cruz, Bolivia?"* I thought, confused. And then I saw them, my beloved girls, quietly sleeping among the warm comforters on my friend's basement suite in Denver, Colorado. Vanessa was 12 and Valerie was 9 years old. True to our family tradition, they had been attending Colegio Aleman (the German School) in Santa Cruz, enjoying the afternoons at our condo's swimming

---

51. Isaiah 49:9

pool, weekends with their cousins at a little lake by the river—a new subdivision my brother Chacho was developing, Laguna Azul. Accompanied by my helper at home, Mariela, on Wednesday afternoons the girls would walk to English lessons at the Centro Boliviano Americano, CBA, the Bolivian American Center. On Tuesdays they would take a regularly scheduled taxicab to their swimming lessons at the Urbari Racquet Club; and on Thursdays they would walk with Mariela to their odontologist to adjust their braces.

Those were carefree days for the girls. In the meantime, I worked an average of 12-hour days, many times including Sundays, and their father worked 14-hour days, always including Saturdays. Sabbath School consisted of a small group of seven girls, including their cousins, Carolina, Ingrid, and Helga; and two other girls Daniella and Debora—Tupi's daughter who used to be in my childhood Sabbath School class.

Otherwise, their social life was around classmates' birthdays. The invitations began to arrive as Vanessa's classmates were turning 13 years old—oh, the beginning of their teens, which meant the parties involved dancing in a poorly lit room. *"Dancing in the darkness?"*—I thought to myself. Yes, the classmates' mothers didn't see the harm, while I was shocked, horrified about exposing our young ones to carnal temptations at such a young age.

*"Oh, dear Lord, please protect my daughters, please keep them away from the evil one. Please lead me to a place where*

*they can stay pure, and safe, and learn more about you, and would want to love you and follow you, and have a Christian education.*" My prayer for my girls' souls and salvation, and an environment where they could receive Christian education became my obsession.

Back in 1983, when Hugo and I got married, we lived in Denver Colorado, where Hugo was going to college and Vanessa was later born. In 1986, we moved to Loma Linda, California, so I could continue my education. Valerie was born in Loma Linda in 1989. In the meantime, back in Bolivia, our parents were getting old. After my dad's passing in 1993, Hugo and I decided to move to Bolivia in 1994. It would allow the girls an opportunity to be with their grandparents, meet their cousins, solidify their Spanish, and learn our culture.

In Denver, our beloved friends were Nick and Angel, who had two children, Jamie and Athena, pretty much our daughters' ages. Our souls were knitted together with this loving couple. While on my knees in the summer of 1998 praying for my girls' Christian education and safe environment, I felt a strong impression to spend their summer school break in Denver, Colorado. The Bolivian school year goes from February to October, with summer break from November to January. Hugo supported my decision, we asked Nick and Angel if we could spend the summer (winter months in the U.S.) with them, and they welcomed us with opened arms. Once in Denver, Vanessa was enrolled at the area Middle School and Valerie at the Elementary

School. To Vanessa's shock, their classmates were into open sex conversations, drinking, and drugs.

*"Oh, dear Lord, please protect my daughters, please keep them away from the evil one. Please lead me to a place where they can stay pure, and safe, and learn more about you, and would want to love you and follow you, and have a Christian education."* This had been the prayer before going to sleep on Tuesday, November 24, 1998. The Lord's prompting at 4:00 AM in the morning couldn't let me sleep any longer. *"Marlene,* was His soft voice, *get ready to study your Bible, I have a message for you."*

*"Then the* Lord *said to Moses: "I am making a covenant with you. Before all your people I will do wonders never before done in any nation in all the world. The people you live among will see how awesome is the work that I, the* Lord, *will do for you."*[52] The Bible Study for the week and this particular day centered around the Israelites on their way to Canaan, the promised land. Moses is begging the Lord to go with them, *"Moses bowed to the ground at once and worshiped. "Lord," he said, "if I have found favor in your eyes, then let the Lord go with us."*[53]

On one hand, the Lord took the Israelites out of Egypt, an idolatrous nation. He had led them through the Red Sea where He miraculously opened a path amidst the waters for their salvation, using Moses as their leader. The Israelites had camped at Mount Sinai where the 10 Commandments

---

52. Exodus 34:10
53. Exodus 34:8, 9

had been presented to this wandering nation; but the Israelites rebelled. Moses went back to Mount Sinai to chisel in stone a new set of tablets because he had broken out of anger the previous ones which had been engraved by the Finger of God. Moses was feeling the burden of leading his people. He relied on God and did not want the journey to the promised land unless the Lord went with them. True to His Word, the Lord pledged to be at the vanguard. He assured miracles no nation had ever seen before. He commanded Moses to leave the place and go.

As I was studying my Bible, I stopped and prayed, *"Jesus, where should I go, where do you want us to go?"* Studying Exodus 34 impressed strongly in me I had to move to another place where my daughters would enjoy the Christian education I was praying for. *"How should I support my girls?"*—was my next question. To my stupefaction, the next verse in the Bible study was in Isaiah, *"So do not fear, for I am with you; do not be dismayed, for I am your God. I will strengthen you and help you; I will uphold you with my righteous right hand."*[54] Deep silence and peace followed— *"What does the Lord want of me, where do you want me to go, Oh Lord?"* I continued praying as I left to work.

*"Marlene, Marlene, you have a phone call and need to go to Human Resources to take your call."* This was the Human Resources Manager who found me in the ladies' room washing my hands. Personal phone calls were strictly pro-

---

54. Isaiah 41:10

hibited by this employer. We had telephones on our desk only for outgoing phone calls to customers. Somehow my loyal friend Charo in Berrien Springs, Michigan, looked up the phone number and called me. *"Kitticita?*—was her voice on the other side of the line. *You need to come to Berrien Springs, Michigan, immediately. My husband Dan went to the Human Resources office at Andrews University with your resume. Someone just presented her resignation, and you are a person who fits the profile they are looking for. We scheduled an appointment for you for next Tuesday, December 1, with Linda Wysong, the Human Resources Director at 10:00 AM. She's a very nice lady; you will do very good."*

Aha, the response to my prayer at 4:30 AM early that morning had an answer at 10:00 AM—the Lord had been preparing me. After celebrating Thanksgiving on Thursday, November 26, with Angel's loving family, Vanessa, Valerie, and I took the 22 hour Greyhound bus trip to South Bend, Indiana, where Dan and Charo were waiting for us. The girls knew about my prayers and Bible study, the Lord's soft voice, listening to his message, following His lead, and also wondered what His plans were for us.

Those were the days prior to all electronic and fast communication we now enjoy, even so, Hugo and I spoke about moving to Berrien Springs, MI. While the girls and I were with Nick and Angel, Hugo's parents were also in Denver on personal business. We spoke about this decision and Mrs. Emma Jorgensen, my beloved mother-in-law, came to say good-bye at the Denver Greyhound bus station. She gave each girl $20 for their trip. After paying for the bus tickets and food, we arrived at South Bend, Indiana, bus station with just $30 in my pocket. No winter clothes for the frigid Michigan winter, no home, no car to go to work with—we only had the promises of *"I am making a covenant with you. Before all your people I will do wonders never before done in any nation in all the world. The people you live among will see how awesome is the work that I, the LORD, will do for you,"* [55] therefore, *"do not fear, for I am with you; do not be dismayed, for I am your God. I will strengthen you and help you; I will uphold you with my righteous right hand."*[56]

It has been over 23 years since I heard the voice of the Lord. True to his promises, He blessed all three of us. The girls received their Christian education through a series of miracles. And the 30 dollars in my pocket, they are still there to help those in need—somehow, they get replenished. And the Lord's soft voice I learned is not only for Bible times, but also real for you and me.

In March of 2022, I met artist James Coleman, an animation legend who used to work for Disney. James shared a story when he was 19 years old. He began working in the mailroom at the Disney Studios. His love for art had already begun and began painting. Mr. Roy Disney saw James's first picture; he liked it so much and purchased it for $30. It gave James the confidence to continue painting, becoming later one of the most famous background paint-

---

55. Exodus 34:10
56. Isaiah 41:10

ers of the most loved Disney films of all times, before pursuing a career as a fine artist.[57] James's art sells all around the world for several thousand dollars. James needed to feel the encouragement of a person like Roy Disney to pursue his dreams and unleashing the artistry within him. Jesus was sold for 30 pieces of silver to save us, and thanks to His death we have been redeemed from sin. I needed the trust from a faithful friend that helped my girls and me in a time of need. The $30 dollars in my pocket was the beginning of a blessed journey, also sowing blessings to those in need.

Jesus has been faithful to his promises.

---

57. https://www.parkwestgallery.com/artist/james-coleman/

## 11. Wonders Never Done Before — The Years at Andrews University

*"Leave your country and your people."*[58]

The clock said 12:00 noon on Friday, December 4, 1998. I kept looking at my watch hour-by-hour and no phone call came. *"Andrews University closes it offices at noon,"* I thought. The clock said 1:00 PM, no phone call. 2:00 PM, still no call. Around 3:00 PM my friend Dan said, *"Linda works late hours, she might be still calling you."* Around 4:00 PM I was losing hope; the winter days in Michigan were short, and Seventh-day Adventist people don't work after sundown.

*"Marlene,"* was the voice on the other side of the phone, *"this is Linda Wysong. We were impressed with your interview and would like to offer you the position of Benefits Specialist. You may want to think it over this weekend and call me back."* Linda was the Human Resources Director at Andrews University, I had interviewed with her on Tuesday, December 1, 1998, and had a follow-up group interview on

---

58. Genesis 12:1

Thursday. Linda had mentioned she was going to call me back on Friday with an answer. My excitement was great when hearing her voice around 4:15 PM. *"Yes,"* was my immediate response, "I accept the offer."

*"By the way,"* she added, *"your reference, Tim, said if you don't get the job you should call him and he will hire you immediately."*

Providing Vanessa and Valerie a Christian education was the goal of our journey and going to be difficult. Soon after our arrival in Berrien Springs, Michigan, while staying with our friends Dan and Charo, we went on Monday, November 30, to enroll the girls at the local church school. I still had $30 in my pocket and providing them the much-desired Christian education was an impossible dream. First we went to the Seventh-day Adventist Village School, highly recommended by our friends. Their responses were that they didn't have any room for any new 4th Graders (Valerie's) class, and that for 7th Grade they would have an opening in January since a student was relocating out of state.

Next were the fees, $300/month, plus all additional enrollment fees. *"What do you do when you don't have money?"* was my thoughtless question. Another person listening to the conversation responded, *"Then, you take your daughters to public school,"* followed by mocking laughter. The sensitive School Secretary, Pam, asked me if I was working and inquired more about our situation. *"Marlene, call me if you get the job at Andrews for they do provide tuition assistance."*

In the meantime, we went to the public schools. Valerie was welcomed at the elementary school and she immediately felt very special. When we arrived at the public middle school, Vanessa refused to be enrolled. For days she cried in her room, praying, and challenging me, *"You said, mom, that the Lord spoke to you just as He spoke to Moses. Have you lost your faith? If he provided manna in the desert for the Israelites, He could provide for my Christian education."*

Getting the job at Andrews University was the beginning of a series of miracles. The next Monday, December 7, I called Pam at the Village school and said I got the job at Andrews. Her response was, *"Great, Marlene. I shared Vanessa's story of faith and desire for Christian education. Two families have come forward and are willing to help. Of the $300 monthly tuition, Andrews University will assist with $100, the two families with $50 each, another $100, and your payment will be $100. Would that work?"* By the time Vanessa started 7th grade in January 1999 at the Village School, her class teacher, Mr. Davidson, had told all her classmates the story of "the little girl of faith," and that is how many people remembered her at that time.

When the next school year began, it was time for Valerie to enter 5th grade, a loving family realized that Vanessa had a sister, and she was going to public school. The Wilsons took Valerie under their wings to ensure she also entered the Village School and received a Christian education.

The Lord continued blessing Vanessa through her high

school academy years. After weeks of prayers, we were impressed she should attend Great Lakes Adventist Academy (GLAA) in Cedar Lake, Michigan. The cost was very high and once again we took the step of faith. While babysitting a nine-month-old boy, the Star family got to love Vanessa and sent an annual contribution to GLAA. To our mutual surprise their employer matched their generous contribution 2-1 and other students were also able to benefit from it. Years later, even Valerie was blessed by this loving and generous family.

Our days at Andrews University were blessed by multiple miracles, finding housing, buying a car, purchasing winter clothes, and all the normal human necessities. Day by day the Lord provided for our needs. The blessings included worshiping at the Pioneer Memorial Church, listening to Dwight Nelson every Sabbath, attending the Christmas concerts, including the Messiah, observing the girls blossom in their activities, including Valerie playing the flute at the school orchestra — all was wonderful. The Lord had been true to His promises.

At work, all seemed wonderful. I had taken the position of Benefits Specialist and within three months was promoted to Assistant Human Resources Director. There was a lot of work in the department, it was baptism by fire trying to learn the nuisances of the responsibilities this new position entailed. Soon I discovered a professional ceiling in which I was stuck. *"Marlene, you don't even have a bachelor's degree, you cannot... you cannot... you cannot,"* were the phrases I constantly heard, even though the work of a professional was being executed.

At night my cries would go up to heaven with the usual lament *"Why me, oh Lord. You knew I wanted to study, you knew I was a good student, you knew ... you didn't ... why me?"* Suddenly I felt and heard a strong voice, *"Stop it."* My Faithful Friend Jesus led me to study his Word. Jesus was visiting Jerusalem and saw a paralytic man complaining that no one helped him to heal. Jesus said to him, *"Rise, take up your bed and walk."*[59] Jesus's message was clear, it did not only apply for the paralytic man at the pool of Bethesda, and it also applied to me. I had allowed my commiseration to paralyze my professional development. *"Rise, take up your bed and walk. Stop feeling sorry for yourself and do something about it,"* were the words I needed to hear.

Immediately I enrolled at Bethel University in Mishawaka, Indiana. Within 18 months I was graduating summa cum laude with a degree in organizational management. Listening and obeying Jesus's words changed my life. It required sacrifice, going to school every Wednesday evening for four hours between 6:00 PM — 10:00 PM. Spending Sunday mornings studying and writing research papers while the girls did their own schoolwork, and many times studying until late hours or getting up very early. Our life's journey might not be easy, yet we have a faithful Friend ready and willing to take our burdens with Him. *"Come to*

---

59. John 5:8

*me, all you who are weary and burdened, and I will give you rest."*[60]

In those days, Andrews University had started the Leadership program and was allowing students to get their PhD by only having a bachelor's degree. Andrews provided scholarships for the university faculty; I wasn't one. I wasn't even a director, only—at this time I had already been promoted to the Associate Director of Human Resources. Full of courage I approached Dr. Andreasen, the University President. *"Dr. Andreasen,"* I said, *"I have learned about your leadership program and how you are teaching now at Newbold College in England. I would like to suggest that this program could also be taught in Latin America. In order to create the program in Latin America, you would need a bilingual leader. That leader could be me; however, in order for me to be the leader, I would need to have my PhD in Leadership. Would you please sponsor my degree?"*

Dr. Andreasen looked at me with a smile and responded, *"Marlene, why are you limiting yourself to Latin America? Why not have this program around the world? Go for it!"* A couple of years later, I was graduating from Andrews University with the Master's Degree in Leadership. When Dr. Andreasen gave me my diploma during the graduation ceremony, he looked in my eyes and said, *"Keep studying, you need to finish your doctoral degree."* I did not continue with the PhD because of my full-time work obligations.

---

60. Matthew 11:28

The phone rang unexpectedly on a Sunday afternoon, February 2003. *"Marlene, this is Dr. Randal Wisbey, President of Columbia Union College (currently Washington Adventist University). You were referred to me for the position of Human Resources Director—our current employee went on maternity leave and is not coming back. I would like to invite you for an interview."*

The years at Andrews University had been blessed, *"How could I leave this place, oh Lord? You brought us here, this is Canaan, this is the promised land."* The time in this place was coming to an end. We had a new Human Resources director at work, so many things were different. *"Should I move because Linda is no longer here? Should I stay and continue helping the employees and those in need?"* Days of prayers and agony followed, I was certain Andrews University was the promised land.

As in years past, the sweet voice of my friend, Jesus, explained to me His plans. *"Marlene,"* He whispered, *"you are only 'a foreigner and stranger on this earth, the land you are longing for is a better country—a heavenly one.[61]" Go,"* Jesus said, and guided me to read his promises on Abraham in Genesis 12. *"The LORD had said to Abram, Go from your country, your people, and your father's household to the land I will show you. [2] "I will make you into a great nation, and I will bless you; I will make your name great, and you will be a bless-*

---

61. Hebrews 11: 13, 16

*ing. ³ I will bless those who bless you, and whoever curses you I will curse; and all peoples on earth will be blessed through you."*[62]

With mixed emotions I left the place I had considered the promised land. The cloud had moved, it was time to find a new settlement, be a blessing to new people, while learning from them. I'm still learning to make the place of my temporary inhabitance a little bit of heaven on earth, wherever I am. I am also longing for our final Promised Land where there shall be no more separation and good-byes. In the meantime, Jesus is always at our side.

---

62. Genesis 12: 1-3

# 12. At Lake Michigan — The Burning Bush

*"Take off your sandals, for the place where you are standing is holy ground."*[63]

One of the most beautiful places to visit in Southwest Michigan are the shores of the lake bearing its name, by the quaint city of St. Joseph. This area is also embellished by marvelous forests where visitors can enjoy walking and hiking among the majestic maple trees, white oaks, poplars, and the colorful redbuds, plus climbing up the sand dunes that lead to Lake Michigan. Although the winters are fierce with excessive snowstorms, springtime arrives with indescribable beauty as plants explode with blooms everywhere, birds chirp, and the sun begins to warm up the fields and the spirits. In the meantime, as the waters from Lake Michigan begin to swelter, they are clamoring for company around their shores in the summer months. The frantic activities by the lake during the exotic summer

---

63. Exodus 3:5

is followed by the exuberant autumn presenting a luscious pageantry of colors.

One of my favorite Sabbath activities was hiking on Warren Dunes or Grand Mere State Parks. The trails on the undeveloped woods of Grand Mere with their unimaginable sand dunes were a great place to find solace. One evening, as the sun was beginning to hide on the horizon, I was seating at the peak of a sand dune, looking west to the lake and enjoying the colors of the crepuscule, a unique bush called my attention. All the leaves were green, full of the summer chlorophyll, yet the tree irradiated bright red colors. The phenomenon caught my eyes, I contemplated it to understand its splendor. At that very moment the location of the setting sun was exactly behind the bush, creating the illusion of a burning bush.

My mind began to wonder and reflect of the encounter Moses had in front of a burning bush that was not being consumed, nor was it a natural sensation. While Moses stood silently contemplating the strange sight, He heard the voice of the Lord calling his name and saying, *"Take off your sandals, for the place where you are standing is holy ground."*[64] Hmmm, Moses was standing on holy ground, and he did not even know it. That evening on the sand dunes of Lake Michigan, the place became my holy ground where I would go and commune with my Friend Jesus who knows me by name.

---

64. Exodus 3:5

The encounter between Moses and His Friend Jesus was not much a time for frivolity. The Lord had a transformational mission for Moses to lead. The Lord's heart was aching because of the misery His people were enduring in Egypt. He was concerned for their suffering. Therefore, He came down to save them and for this reason the Lord needed Moses. Is that so? Yes, the story is beautifully described in Exodus 3, sharing with Moses in compassionate words:

> *"I have indeed seen the misery of my people in Egypt. I have heard them crying out because of their slave drivers, and I am concerned about their suffering. So, I have come down to rescue them from the hand of the Egyptians and to bring them up out of that land into a good and spacious land, a land flowing with milk and honey—the home of the Canaanites, Hittites, Amorites, Perizzites, Hivites and Jebusites. And now the cry of the Israelites has reached me, and I have seen the way the Egyptians are oppressing them. Go now, go. I am sending you to Pharaoh to bring my people, the Israelites, out of Egypt."*[65]

Moses response was of self-doubt and pity, *"Who am I?"*[66] he asked the Lord. Had not Moses spent 40 years in the desert of Midian, close to Mount Sinai, taking care of sheep while communing with the Lord? Was this not the self-assured Moses that as a young prince understood his mission in life to be the liberator of the Israelites in Egypt

---

65. Exodus 3: 7-10
66. Exodus 3:11

taken them away from slavery and bondage to Pharaoh? Is this the same person?

With infinite love and patience his Friend Jesus had been working in Moses' heart and now was the time to take action and help "the least of these." But God didn't push, nor did He command like the slave masters would do. God was not disappointed nor used brutal force. With His loving and gentle voice, He only said to Moses, *"I will be with you."*[67]

*"I will be with you,"* where the words and I needed to hear constantly from Jesus during those days when I lived in Michigan. Although I worked in a small community, hundreds of people circulated the grounds of Andrews University every day, yet I felt lonely. In my Human Resources role, I helped multiple people during the week, yet on weekends I felt forsaken, alone. Sadness was a constant companion that I pushed aside with solitary walks by the beautiful lake. Although my face might have reflected joy, my soul felt abandoned. Until one friend said to me, *"Marlene, this might be your Arabia experience."* The words were referring to the days that Paul spent in the desert of Arabia learning directly from the Lord. And here, sitting on the tip of a sand dune by Lake Michigan, observing the sun setting behind a single bush, the Lord brought my attention to His message to Moses in front of a burning shrub. Looking back, oh how I wish I would have heard God's

---

67. Exodus 3:12

voice, not necessarily *"I will be with you,"* but *"Marlene, I am with you."*

There are times when we don't hear His voice, *"I will be with you,"* instead we hear sadness, loneliness, desperation. We just need to stop and pay close attention to God's words that are sufficient for our lives, may we always hear them and trust in Him, our forever Friend.

*"I will be with you. Today, tomorrow, and always, I am with you."*

## 13. Experiencing Joy — Who is my Husband?

*"Ecclesiastes names thee Almighty, the Maccabees name thee Creator, the Epistle to the Ephesians names thee Liberty, Baruch names thee Immensity, the Psalms name thee Wisdom and Truth, John names thee Light, the Book of Kings names thee Lord, Exodus names thee Providence, Leviticus Sanctity, Esdras Justice, creation names thee God, man names thee Father; but Solomon names thee Compassion, which is the most beautiful of all thy names."*[68]

*"Since both of you love each other so much, I now declare you husband and wife."* Those were the words of my future brother-in-law, José Luis Santa Cruz, one warm, sunny, Sabbath afternoon at the church's backyard. I was 16 years old and my friend, Hugo, the son of the church pastor was 15. Hugo had his group of friends and girlfriends his own age, yet he would constantly come to me, caress me, and then

---

68. Hugo, Victor. *Les Misérables, p.40, Release Date May 1994, eBook #135.*

go back to play with his friends. In the meantime, spending
time with my sister Coqui and her boyfriend (later fiancé
and husband) was my pastime, trying to evade a galán that
was trying to persuade me and was highly encouraged to
date me. José Luis was studying theology and as a future
church minister, he would perform weddings. He decided
to practice with Hugo and me during one of Hugo's multiple stops to tell me he loved me. It didn't bother me or
concern me since, as he was one year younger, I considered
him a boy.

*"And now I declare you husband and wife,"* were the words
of Pastor Jorgensen as he was marrying his son Hugo and
me seven years later at the same church. It was the culmi-
nation of my dream and prayers, marrying a Christian person and the son of the church pastor. Up until that point of
my life, all I wanted was a Christ-centered home. A book
recommended to begin preparing for raising children 20
years before they were born. At age 17 when I read that
book, my spiritual preparation began. Oh, how I longed
for the moment to have my own Christian home and to be
happy at last!

Being naïve about words and emotions being defined
differently by individuals, soon after our wedding I realized that for Hugo being happy meant going to parties,
spending time with friends while drinking. *"Why did you
marry me?"* I asked Hugo after this severe shock. *"Because I
thought you wanted to do the things your father didn't allow you
to do,"* was his response.

Obviously, there was a huge misunderstanding on both of our sides. To his credit, he had been forced to be the exemplary externally religious pastor's son, and as an adult he rebelled against it. While the lack of open conversations about Christ growing up had led me to desire even more to have a Christ-loving husband. Hugo and I were married for 16 years, we had two lovely daughters into whom my love was poured. Hugo is now happily married to a lady that understands him, and the Lord blessed me as well with a loving husband.

Why are some people happy and others seem to live in a continuous state of unhappiness? Several clinical studies can be done. It could be an excellent topic for a PhD thesis. Psychologist debate about it; people seek counseling, yet there is still plenty of unhappiness in this world. It was inexplicable why my dad would denote a constant deep sadness, yet I didn't observe the same countenance in mom — she was energetic, stressed, and assertive; but I don't remember mamá on a constant stage of sadness as I remember dad.

Several books have been written about happiness. I once read *The Happiness Project* by Gretchen Rubin. The author began chronicling for 12 months her decisions and deliberate actions to be happy. It became a New York Times' best seller and in 2018, a 10th anniversary revised edition was published.

Even more perplexing, billions of dollars are spent every year by people around the world of all races and creeds seeking happiness. In their wrong search for happiness, many times they reach extreme sadness, sickness, and even death. Some people confuse happiness with pleasure, they seek happiness in the wrong places, engage in wrong activities, consuming palliatives and substances that would provide a short-lived indulgence. There is a difference between temporal happiness and continuous joy.

What is joy? *"Commonly joy is understood as a feeling of pleasure or happiness that comes from success, good fortune, or a sense of well-being."* Merriam Webster dictionary.

What is Joy in the Bible? An article by Words of Faith Hope Love says:

> *"Joy is an essential component of the Christian life, and it appears over a hundred times in the Bible, it describes a feeling of happiness, and it differs in significant ways. Joy in the Hebrew uses two words, simchah [sim-khaw'], which means joy, gladness, or mirth. Then there is the word sason [saw-sone'], which means exultation or rejoicing. It is derived from the root word sus [soos], which is a verb meaning to exult or rejoice.v"*[69]
>
> *"The most prevalent word in Greek for joy is chara [khar-ah']. Its first occurrence is about the nativity of Jesus in Matthew 2:10, which says, "when they saw the star, they rejoiced exceedingly with great joy." Chara means joy, calm delight, or inner gladness. It is related to chairo [khah'-ee-ro], which means to rejoice and charis [khar'-ece], which means grace.*

---

69. *"What is Joy in the Bible?"* December 1, 2019 blog. https://www.wordsoffaith-hopelove.com/what-is-joy-in-the-bible/

*Therefore, chara means to rejoice because of grace. It is the
awareness of God's grace or favors through Jesus, as well as
our reaction to it.*

*Studying these words lets us understand that biblical joy
comes from the Lord. It is a perpetual gladness of the heart
that comes from knowing, experiencing, and trusting Jesus.
Martin Lloyd-Jones said, "joy, in other words, is the response
and the reaction of the soul to a knowledge of the Lord Jesus
Christ." Moreover, biblical joy is not based on our possessions
or circumstances like worldly joy. It is "that inward peace and
sufficiency that is not affected by outward circumstances."* [70]

Without knowing the Hebrew or Greek roots for the
word joy, my personal definition of joy is the sense of
Christ's presence in my life that combines a feeling of
peace (His presence) with inner gladness (experiencing His
presence). In other words, my joy, which is a deep internal
feeling of gladness and peace, is dependent on the Spirit
of Jesus abiding in my soul. Joy does not equal pleasure,
which is the temporal gratification of a selfish desire. Joy is
a present from the Lord because it is something we cannot
obtain by ourselves We don't buy it with money—it was
given to us through the gift of His blood. Because joy is
not superficial and external, it is the reflection of His peace
and presence in our lives. It cannot be faked. Joy is one of
the biggest blessings with which a person can be rewarded.

---

70. *Idem*

The Book of John records the words of Jesus saying, *"I
have told you these things so that my joy may be in you and
that your joy may be complete."[71]* What was Jesus referring
to? In John 15, Jesus is talking to His disciples about being dependent on Him. Jesus uses the analogy of the vine
and the branches. In a vine, the branches are completely
depending on the nourishment they get from the one vine;
and with that nourishment we can enjoy the fruits of the
vine through the branches. In other words, right before his
crucifixion, Jesus was telling His disciples that as long as
we grasp tightly to Him, we would experience joy. Yes, we
may suffer, but despite the suffering we would be joyful.
Ah! This explains why so many of the Christian martyrs
when burned at the stake were singing. Physically they
were suffering, emotionally they were experiencing the joy
that only comes from holding tight to Christ.

In Galatians the apostle Paul says, *"But the fruit of the
Spirit is love, joy, peace, patience, kindness, goodness, faithfulness..."[72]* OK, joy is a fruit of the Spirit, which means joy
(inner peace and gladness) is not something I obtain by my
own efforts or merits, it is rather a fruit of the Spirit. Just
like the vine that produces fruits through the branches as
long as the branch remains connected to the vine.

Before enumerating the fruits of the Spirit, the apostle
Paul says in Galatians 5: 16 and 18:

---

71. John 15:11
72. Galatians 5:22

*"... walk by the Spirit or being led by the Spirit..., be led by the Spirit." What does "walking by the Spirit mean?*

*"In ancient Judaism, the term "walk" referred to the way in which one conducts their life. Walking was often associated with the law. So, Paul flips this around and instead of calling believers to conduct their lives according to the law, he tells them to conduct their lives according to the Spirit... When we walk by the Spirit, we do not end up living out the works of the flesh. Instead, the fruit of the Spirit becomes evident in our lives. Walking by the Spirit means looking to Jesus for our direction. It is a daily journey of asking ourselves, "What does the Lord want me to do today? What will honor and please him?" It involves examining our lives and if we recognize the works of the flesh within us, we repent and ask for the Spirit's help."[73]*

Jesus was extremely thoughtful and compassionate. First, He taught His disciples how their joy could be complete — by grasping to Him just like the branches are tightly connected to the branch. Then He prayed to the Father for us *"... I pray for them... those you have given me... so that they may have the full measure of my joy in them... "[74]* He also said to His disciples about His Substitute on this earth, the Holy Spirit, and finally He says that as long as we have the

---

73. *"What does it Mean to Walk by the Spirit?"* https://dailyshepursues.com/walk-by-the-spirit/#:~:text=Walking%20by%20the%20Spirit%20means%20following%20the%20Spirit's%20lead.&text=So%20Paul%20flips%20this%20around,lives%20according%20to%20the%20Spirit.
74. John 17:9, 13

Holy Spirit with us, then we can experience that divine joy that comes only from Him.

Going through a divorce is not easy, it rips the soul apart, because the sacred union became *"one flesh."*[75] But now it is being torn—oh, what a painful process. It was in the middle of night when my tears had me breathless, when I experienced Jesus embrace and His sweet words in Isaiah, *"For your Maker is your Husband—the Lord Almighty is His Name."*[76] Oh man, why hadn't I seen this verse before? Right there, in front of me was the perfect husband, the one I had always prayed for, one who would always be by my side. At that point, when I began to experience and trust Jesus as my husband, then I began *"to taste and see that the Lord is good."*[77] My Maker and Husband made me feel special and filled my heart with joy.

During a Sabbath meal one of my male guests asked me, *"Marlene, when is your husband coming home? Is he going to join us for lunch?"*

*"Oh*—was my response, *I don't have a husband."*

His immediate response was, *"I am so sorry, I thought you were married."*

*"Actually…"* I replied, *"I do have a Husband, For my Maker is my Husband. And I feel sorry for you guys because He cannot be your wife."*

All the guests laughed, and my guest responded, *"Mar-*

---

75. Genesis 2:24
76. Isaiah 54:5
77. Psalm 34:8

*lene, the Greek word used in Isaiah is neutral, it could be masculine or feminine, therefore, the Lord could also be my wife."* Everyone at the dinner table was silent and pondering on the word. My Maker is everything to me.

What else can I ask? Why should I seek worldly pleasure when my soul is full of His constant joy (perfect peace and gladness?)

*"And now I declare you husband and wife."* When I met Jesus as my husband *"For your Maker is your husband—the LORD Almighty is his name... "[78]*, only then my joy became complete because He gave me the full measure of His true love.

Victor Hugo said, *"Ecclesiastes names Thee Almighty, the Maccabees name Thee Creator, the Epistle to the Ephesians names Thee Liberty, Baruch names Thee Immensity, the Psalms name Thee Wisdom and Truth, John names Thee Light, the Book of Kings names Thee Lord, Exodus names Thee Providence, Leviticus Sanctity, Esdras Justice, creation names Thee God, man names Thee Father; but Solomon names Thee Compassion, which is the most beautiful of all thy names."[79]* Moses names Thee Compassionate and Gracious, Loving and Faithful, and Forgiving. To me, He is my Father, my Friend, and my beloved Husband.

---

78. Isaiah 54:5
79. Hugo, Victor. *Les Misérables, p.40, Release Date May 1994, eBook #135.*

# 14. Being Like Jesus — My Dear Vanessa

*"Keep me as the apple of your eye; hide me*
*under the shadow of your wings."*[80]

*"Dear Father, please help Vanessa to be like Jesus. In your Holy Name we pray, Amen."* My constant prayer with Vanessa when she was a little girl was, *"Dear Lord, please help Vanessa to be like Jesus."* Vanessa was around four years old and to my amazement one evening as soon as I said, *"Amen,"* Vanessa looked deeply into my eyes and said, *"Mom, if you want me to be like Jesus, you need to pray to be like Mary."* Wow, how thoughtful that a little girl would be so profound and know that children learn best by example. Jesus learned to love God through the exemplary life of His mother Mary, His best teacher.

Vanessa instilled in me a deeper desire to learn from the Source that Mary learned to be a loving mother and Spirit-guided teacher. *"Dear Lord, please help Vanessa to be like Jesus, and help me to be a good mother as Mary,"* those were my new prayers. Children want their parents to be perfect as they grow up and realize that the ones they admire and

---

80. Psalm 17:8

trust the most are not as perfect as they thought, they get disappointed and many times rebel against the family, their social circle, and even God. In like manner, parents put excessive pressure wanting their children to be perfect, which also causes mutual frustration, rejection, and flagrant disobedience.

False expectations are the root of unexpected and unwanted behaviors. When expectations are set with clear guidance, the behavior is mostly congruent to the expectation. As a child, I expected Vanessa (and later Valerie as well) to love Jesus. As adults, I expected them and provided the training, environment, and education to love Jesus, to be responsible individuals, and then be successful professionals. As a parent, Vanessa expected me to be like the ideal mother of a perfect child.

But what *is to be* perfect? Growing up I felt my Teutonic parents wanted me to be flawless and irreproachable like my older siblings were. In the gospel of Matthew, Jesus said, *"Be perfect, therefore, as your heavenly Father is perfect."*[81] Somehow, I felt Matthew 4:48 was my mother's favorite Bible verse, and as she said those words to me I can still see her finger pointing at me, her stern eyes looking directly to me, and her assertive command to be perfect.

On Wednesday evenings during prayer meetings one of my mother's friends used to pray, *"Dear Father in heaven, please remove the spiderwebs from my heart."* After weeks and

---

81. Matthew 4:48

months of listening to the same plea, finally my mother asked at the end of the prayer, *"Sister, why don't you pray for the Father to kill the spider of your heart?"* That was my mother — no excuses, just results, just *be* perfect.

What did Jesus mean when He said, *"Be perfect, therefore, as your heavenly Father is perfect?"*

It happened on a beautiful sunny, warm, and breezy day on a mountain — we know it as the Sermon on the Mount. Jesus was surrounded by a multitude of followers. Due to the size of the crowd, He sat on the mountain top so His voice could be echoed and heard by all. And then Jesus began to talk. As I reflect on this scene, it seems to me Jesus was not so much in a teaching or preaching mode, Jesus was in a reflection mode. I can imagine Jesus thinking about the character of God and sharing with the crowds the goodness of the Lord. Jesus was encouraging His listeners by showering them with blessings or the greatest outpouring of his desire for us to be like His Father — humble, comforting, meek, thirsting for righteousness, merciful, pure in heart, and peacemakers. Providing the delicious flavor of a life with the Lord and shining that delight to others around us. And finally, loving and praying for those who hate us.

In Matthew 5 we read:

*He said:*
   *[3] "Blessed are the poor in spirit, for theirs is the kingdom of heaven.*

What Jesus actually was trying to say was *"My Father has a poor spirit. When you are humble as He is, you will be happy."*

*⁴ Blessed are those who mourn, for they will be comforted.*

In other words, *"My Father is the perfect Comforter. When you are sad, He will comfort you. And when you feel his loving consolation, you will be happy. Likewise, when you see someone suffering and you comfort them, you are being like my Father—and that brings you happiness."*

*⁵ Blessed are the meek, for they will inherit the earth.*

Meaning, *"My Father is gentle. When you endure injury with patience without resentment as He has, you will be happy."*

*⁶ Blessed are those who hunger and thirst for righteousness, for they will be filled.*

*"My Father has food for you that will satisfy the hunger of your soul. He can provide you the water that will not make you thirsty again. If you deeply desire what He has and is offering you, you will be happy."*

*⁷ Blessed are the merciful, for they will be shown mercy.*

*"My Father is benevolent. When you accept His grace by having a continuous desire to do good, you will be happy."*

*⁸ Blessed are the pure in heart, for they will see God.*

*"My Father has a flawless heart. When you yearn to have his purity, you will be happy."*

*⁹ Blessed are the peacemakers, for they will be called children of God.*

*"My Father brings peace to this world. When you imitate Him, you will be happy."*

*¹⁰ Blessed are those who are persecuted because of righteousness, for theirs is the kingdom of heaven.*

*"My Father knows it will not be easy, but be happy because you will be in His Kingdom in heaven."*

When Jesus pondered about His Father and shared with us the beauty of His character, Jesus then said, *"Be perfect, therefore, as your heavenly Father is perfect."*

Oh, Jesus wants me to be loving, to have the pure spirit of His Heavenly Father, to be an encourager, a good listener, humble, comforting, meek, thirsting, and seeking righteousness, merciful, and a peacemaker. That is the perfection Jesus is talking about. It is not an exterior demonstration of a learned behavior based on human expectations; it is the internal search for the source of perfection based on Divine intervention. It is God living with me; even if I would never achieve perfection, it is an extremely important pursuit. Once I realize what Jesus means with being perfect, then I don't need to worry if I meet anyone's expectations. It is the marvelous epiphany while seeking the presence of my Lord and being showered by His love.

The Greek word in Matthew 4:48 is *teleios* and it can mean 'perfect' but is more usually used to refer to maturity or wholeness.

The moments of solitude spending time with the Lord are short. We then have to face our daily routine. Not everyone around us will delight in the invisible presence of the Lord. As a matter of fact, the demons that possessed pitiful victims when they saw Jesus, they shrieked and

wanted to run away from His presence. Jesus knew his
followers would be persecuted just as He was and prophets before Him were. Jesus smiled and nodded His head,
encouraging us by stating we should actually feel blessed.
Truly? Feel blessed about being persecuted, ridiculed, and
tormented? No, Jesus did not mean that harassment is a
blessing. He said that the rejection that resulted from being
perfect like Him, meant that we had the love of God within us. And His love is deep—even deeper than the deepest
part of the ocean, long—even as the tallest mountain, and
wide—even as wide as the infinite.[82]

I can slowly comprehend what Vanessa wanted from me
as a mom, and what I wanted from her as a girl. Both of us
wanted to be loving—it was the perfection we were both
seeking from one another.

*"Dear Lord, please help Vanessa to be like Jesus, and help me
to be a good mother as Mary."* Vanessa was around 10 years
old one evening as I finished praying. *"Mom,"* she said, *"you
no longer need to say that prayer…"* pause and silence as she
looked deep into my eyes… *"you are already a good mom."*

My praise goes only *"to Him who is able to do immeasurably more than all we ask or imagine, according to his power
that is at work within us."*[83] Being a child as Jesus was or a
mother as Mary was, is not my job. Being like Jesus comes
from *"Him who is able to do immeasurably more than all we
ask or imagine…"*

---

82. Ephesians 3:18
83. Ephesians 3:20

# 15. Resentment — Letting Go of the Cancer that Erodes the Soul

*"Create in me a clean heart, Oh God; and renew a right spirit within me."*[84]

*"Bring your mom the bedsheets,"* was the humoristic phrase dad said to Coqui and me when on some Sundays mom sat to write letters to her children studying abroad. Mom worked as a schoolteacher for two different schools — one in the mornings and the other in the afternoons. She was a very dedicated teacher and wrote her daily study plans in the evenings. In the 1960s — the years before computers, mom hand wrote all the class materials she was going to teach the next day. She did it year after year and fully devoted all her attention as she prepared getting ready for a new day ahead. I can still sense the quiet evenings at home while mom prepared her study plans and dad read or heard the news. Maybe this is the reason why I still enjoy quiet evenings of reading, studying, or writing.

---

84. Psalm 51:10

Howbeit, when the time set aside for mom to write letters to her children, mom was a different person. Sunday
afternoons were generally serene—all the cooking and
cleaning was done; all her school preparation had been
completed. At home everything seemed peaceful, but
inside mom a torrent of pain was flowing. She sat at the
wooden kitchen table, in one hand she held her pen, in the
other a well-ironed white cotton handkerchief. Her usual concentration was noticeable, *"Querido Pepe,"* she would
write, and then the tears began to pour quietly, yet inces-
santly. I think dad's mischievous sentence to bring her a
bedsheet was to calm her down. One handkerchief was not
going to be enough to wipe away the grief of having her
beloved children so far away.

From the distance, I watched mom's sorrow. Her children, her precious grown progeny were studying too far
from her. The letters didn't come soon enough bringing
her the needed balm. It wasn't every Sunday—oh no, too
painful to write letters every weekend! The next day dad
would go to the post office and mail mom's letter (maybe with his own message as well). And then the endless
counting of days began—week one, week two, three, and
so on, waiting to receive a response. Every day dad would
go to the post office looking for a missive from the boys
(Pepe or Buby) in Romania or La Pequeña (Lita, "the little
one," as dad would dearly call her) in La Paz.

Pimpi left for Lima, Peru, in February of 1962 for nursing school. I was only two years old and don't remember her

departure. It was different when Lita took the bus, *"Flota Galgo,"* in January of 1964 on her way to La Paz to study engineering. Seeing the bus leave late in the afternoon, and going back home while holding dad's hand, walking on the dusty unpaved streets, left a feeling of emptiness in our hearts. The departures became more painful as the understanding of a five-year-old girl became acute of what a farewell meant.

Unstoppable tears followed our way two years later after saying good-bye to Pepe. He took the same *"Flota Galgo"* bus to La Paz in February 1965. The itinerary was a stop in La Paz, getting his student visa, and then taking an airplane to Bucharest, Romania, where he had received a full scholarship for an engineering degree. Oh, no, these were the days before the internet and inexpensive cell phone communication. Our farewell meant not seeing Pepe for the next several years! Unlike Lita, who could take a one-day trip back to Santa Cruz for some of her summer breaks, Pepe had left and we didn't know when he was going to return.

Mom continued watching her children leave for college. Buby also left for Romania in September 1968, Chacho to La Paz in January of 1971, and a few months later Chichin to Houston, Texas, on a student exchange program. As her home became emptier, mom had the companion of her two little girls—Coqui and Kitty, who she was going to keep close to her for as long as she could.

Coqui was now 16 years old, and I was 15. *"Señora Rosa,*

*please leave the girls with us. They will continue going to their schools here in Hamburg. We will ensure taking them to church every Sabbath with us. They will go to college; we will take care of them...* "Those were the offers in January 1974 from our beloved friends Clarita and Elizabeth to our mother. Dad was quiet, just observing, he left the decision to mom; but mom was not going to leave her teenage girls in Germany. *"Oh no, they are too young, I will not let go of them at this tender age, oh no, don't ask that of me..."*

Coqui and I returned to Bolivia with our parents in early 1974. Mom was happy and proud having returned home with her girls, but I wasn't. Nothing in Santa Cruz was the same. Our Sabbath School friends, our same age, had been sent to Colegio Adventista del Plata in Argentina. Perly, Lanny, Chichico, Chinita, Tupi and Anita, had all left. In Santa Cruz I was feeling lonely and confused. Soon I met other friends and the desolation subsided, yet an insidious cancer had begun eroding my soul. This ugly and hidden skeleton was resentment.

Although life continued, I kept my secret, *"Why did mom take me back to Santa Cruz,... why didn't I stay with Elizabeth,... why I was deprived of excellent education and the friendship of excellent Christian role models, why, why, why?"* Mom would not answer. *"You are too young,"* she might say at times.

My turn for college came and ended too quickly. In only two years I finished the three-year associate's nutrition program in Montemorelos, Mexico, with flying colors and the hope to get a scholarship for the bachelor's program at Loma Linda University in California. After graduation, my dream was obtaining my PhD and working in research. The future seemed very bright. For the 25-hour and 1,523-mile drive I was able to find a ride with a medical student, a recent graduate who was on his way to Stanford University for his residency, another lady also came along. We took driving turns and would sing on the road to keep each other awake.

The student (let's call him Peter) spoke Spanish, French, and English — the same three languages I spoke; we would sing the same songs in a different language (I still hum them in my head *"Happiness is to know the Savior, living a life within his favor, having a change in my behavior, happiness is the Lord ... "*). Peter had lived in Europe, traveled a lot, and we shared excellent conversations. Somewhere in Arizona, due to the high heat and not watching the vehicle's dashboard, the car stopped — the engine was in flames. Stranded in the desert, a truck driver took all three of us to the next truck stop where we were able to rent a car and look for a hotel to stay for the next few days. It was a long wait until Peter received money to pay to have the car fixed and continue our journey to Loma Linda. Needless to say, by the end of our very long journey, we had developed feelings for one another.

Summer school began soon after my arrival at La Sierra University — the Loma Linda University extension campus. Inorganic, organic, and biochemistry were the three classes I took. In the meantime, Peter continued his trip to Stanford University in San Francisco. He visited me one weekend, we went to church and truly enjoyed our friendship. My joy led me to write three long typed letters to my parents at the college library where they had small booths with typewriters. I shared with them about this amazing person I met. As I was typing and smiling one afternoon, another student looked at me and asked, *"What is so funny?"*

*"Oh,"* I replied, *"it is a letter to my parents."*

*"Let's see if they find it as funny as you do,"* was his impolite and unsolicited comment.

True to this stranger's prediction, my parents didn't find my news about Peter funny at all. It probably took about a week for the letters to reach home and another week for my father to fly to Southern California with my brother Chi-chin to take me back home. Dad and mom were angry, so indignant that there was no reasoning with them. *"You are going home, period! Your mom said to come and get you…"* I could have escaped; I could have hidden at a friend's house in Beverly Hills where she was cleaning homes and she could have helped me find a job. I could have ended all contact with my parents, and they would have no way of finding me.

For whatever reason I didn't do it. A few days later I was taking a plane back to Santa Cruz, Bolivia, with dad and Chichin, where irritated and judging siblings waited. *"You are such a fool… it is your fault…"* were some of the remarks I remember.

What was Peter's sin? None. To my eyes, he was almost perfect. To my family he was different, born in Africa, of African parents and lineage. How sad. *"But mom, didn't you take me as a girl to Sabbath School and taught me the song 'Jesus loves the little children, all the children of the world, red or yellow, black, or white, all are precious in his sight, Jesus loves the children of the world'?"*

No answer. How confusing, *"Didn't you and dad have friends of all races in Germany? Didn't we help and host Indians in our home in Hamburg?"* No answer.

One brother just said, *"it is hard to understand… "*

Shattered dreams, twice in five tender young years. Dreams of my future, of my education, of my love to study. All were gone, twice — the wounds were so deep that woke me up in the middle of the night bathed in tears. Another wasted year of life followed, no goals ahead, just disorientation and incertitude. And the resentment kept creeping in and robbing my inner peace.

Insight comes slowly through adversity. This time I was no longer the teenager with shattered dreams, I was the mom of a teenager with a broken home. To my perplexity, I observed resentment emerging from her soul. As in years past, the sweet voice of my constant and faithful Friend Jesus came to my ears, *"Marlene, Marlene, unless you forgive your mom, you will not be able to be a good mom."* Alas, the secret was to extirpate the cancer corroding my soul, for so many years allowing it to take root.

*"Lord, please forgive me, and help me to forgive mom,"* were

my constant prayers. *"If you confess your sins, he is faithful and just and will forgive us our sins and purify us from unrighteousness."*[85]

Oh, resentment is a sin? How could it be, it is not part one of the Ten Commandments? *"My dear Marlene,"* Jesus would say. *"It is written everywhere in the Bible. Stories of resentment and the horrific results are abundant. Remember how resentful Lucifer was in heaven when he saw the honor God the Father provided to me—and what were the devastating results—being cast out of heaven? Remember the resentment of Cain when his offering was not accepted as Abel's was—and what was the result—murder? Remember Joseph's brothers resentment because of a tender love he received from their old father Jacob—and what were the results—deceit, malice?*

*"Remember Miriam and Aaron being resentful to their brother Moses and what were the results—leprosy? Remember the Pharisees when I came to this earth to give all of you salvation—and what were the results—my crucifixion? Marlene, resentment is the root of many evils, including covetousness and murder which are part of the Ten Commandments. You need to meditate deeper in Galatians 5 mentioning what is contrary to the Spirit—"conflict with one another, hatred, discord, jealousy, fits of rage, selfish ambition, dissensions…" On another note, the fruits of the Spirit are "love, joy peace, patience, forgiveness, kindness, goodness, faithfulness, gentleness and self-control."*

Jesus' voice continued, *"Marlene, I want to give you love,*

---

85. 1 John 1:9

*joy, peace, and forgiveness. Remember when you used to pray to me "Create in me a clean heart of Lord and renew a loyal spirit within me?"[86] Yes Marlene, this is my response, allowing you to see within you the ugliness of resentment that blemishes the heart."*

Jesus wanted to heal my soul and remove the cancer of resentment that was eroding my inner being, He was faithful to the prayer of my German Bible teacher, Frau Schitteck— *"Blessed are the pure in heart for they will see God,"[87]*. His gentle and sweet response occurred at a day and time I don't know when. All I remember are the marvelous years mom and I enjoyed before I caressed her for the last time, free from the pain that resentment had caused. Jesus had been healing my soul. He was creating a clean and pure heart within me.

Now Jesus' words make sense, *"For God so loved the world that He gave His one and only Son, that whoever believes in Him shall not perish but have eternal life."[88]* Jesus is telling me, *"For God so loved Marlene, that He sent Jesus so that she shall not perish but have eternal life."* The beautiful promise is that Jesus loves you too. He came and died for each of us so that you can have everlasting life with Him. Free from pain, free from resentment. Never allow resentment to erode your soul. There is a cure for this cancer. *"When I am lifted up from the earth, I will draw all people to myself."[89]*

---

86. Psalm 51:10
87. Matthew 5:8
88. John 3:16
89. John 12:32

# 16. I Have Called You Friends — Blessed by Friends

*"Love each other as I have loved you."* [90]

*"Of all possessions, a friend is the most precious."* [91]

Our tranquil afternoons after studying biochemistry at La Sierra University in Riverside, California, were followed by moments of meditation and sharing our spiritual discoveries. We cherished the time relating our epiphanies during our private Bible studies. I still remember her peaceful and reflective demeanor, the minutes turning into hours listening to her wise and profound advice. She broke the silence and said, *"Marlene, we need to learn to pray to have good friends. Have you prayed about it? I have learned,"* she continued, *"that we even have to pray so that the Lord will send good friends our way,"* were the words of my sweet friend Lynette.

Lynette's sage advice during our college years is one

90. John 15:12
91. Herodotus

of the reasons why I feel so blessed with my God-loving friends. One employer was very strict about hiring only Christians, until one time that we interviewed a lady who would do an excellent job, yet she was Muslim. We received the approval of hiring her as long as she came through a staffing agency. During her training, I observed that she was very scared. We spoke and finally said, *"Heba, do you believe in the God of Ibrahim?"* She nodded, *"then* –I continued, *we are friends for I also believe in the God of Ibrahim."* Needless to say, we became excellent coworkers until she moved to Egypt. Heba shared her love of God and deep desire of learning more about Him and His Son Jesus.

In John 15 Jesus said to His beloved followers, *"I no longer call you servants, because a servant does not know his master's business. Instead, I have called you friends… "*[92] I think this is one of the most beautiful verses in the Bible, *"… I have called you friends… "*

What is a friend? Hard to define? Yes, because of the different ways people interpret words. Friendship goes beyond words, it is the intimate link between two souls, unshakable regardless of the vicissitudes of life. Friendship is one of the greatest gifts we can receive while alive. It is an unbreakable bond only lost in death. In the Garden of Eden, God would talk to Adam as His friend. Jesus walked around the garden, teaching Adam about the various plants, feeling the different textures, observing the thou-

---

92. John 15:15

sands of color variations, smelling the flowers, delighting in the sweet melodies of the birds, laughing when trying to catch sleeky fishes with their hands, naming the animals while caressing their necks and being licked by doggies. They would lay on the warm grass during the dark hours of the night observing the stars, as Jesus told Adam the story of creation and the universe and various galaxies. Jesus would connect to Adam through nature and develop an inseparable bond. When holy angels had to ban Adam and Eve from the Garden of Eden, Jesus wept in the same way He wept when Lucifer was cast out of heaven and could no longer be redeemed. But even in the great sorrow, Jesus said to His Father, *"I want to see my friend Adam and spend time with him again. I don't want him to perish and have eternal damnation. Oh, dear Father, please allow me to go down to earth and bring my friend back to us."* And God the Father accepted the sacrifice that only a compassionate friend, and His blameless Son could make.

Friendship is the mutual commitment of sharing our vulnerabilities while giving our precious time to a special person we love. Just like in the Garden of Eden, God continues seeking us as His true friend. *"Marlene, is this possible?"* Someone asked me. Oh yes, my dear, it is possible. Remember Enoch? He established a marvelous relationship with the Lord to the point that God would not allow this loving friend to remain on this earth experiencing suffering. Our Lord took Enoch with him to share their forever friendship.

Remember Moses? Moses would go up a mountain to a solitary place to spend time with God, to learn from Him and obtain needed strength for his insecurities and frustrations perpetrated by his followers. Moses would seek God's presence, He spent so much time alone with God that in Exodus we read, *"The Lord would speak to Moses face to face, as one speaks to a friend."* [93]

Even more significant, after spending so much time alone with the Lord, Moses reflected God's holiness, Moses' face was radiant. Exodus 34 says, *[29] "When Moses came down from Mount Sinai with the two tablets of the covenant law in his hands, he was not aware that his face was radiant because he had spoken with the Lord." [30] "When Aaron and all the Israelites saw Moses, his face was radiant, and they were afraid to come near him…" [33] "When Moses finished speaking to them, he put a veil over his face." [34] "But whenever he entered the Lord's presence to speak with him, he removed the veil until he came out…" [35] "they saw that his face was radiant. Then Moses would put the veil back over his face until he went in to speak with the Lord."* [94]

Frequently we have excuses for not spending time with the Lord, we allow spiderwebs growing in our soul due to spiritual neglect. Even worse in this era of high speed and multiple communication channels, we may become too distracted and overlook our only true Friend. We are trapped with excessive yet unimportant communication.

---

93. Exodus 33:11
94. Exodus 34: 29-35

Why did Jesus say, *"I no longer call you servants, because a servant does not know his master's business. Instead, I have called you friends ... ?"*[95] I don't recall the disciples being Jesus' servants anytime during His ministry. Jesus' words had a deeper meaning, servitude to sin. And because we are servants to our sinful nature, Jesus came to redeem us to the true image of God, to transform us by His power, love, and friendship back to the original plan of being friends with Jesus as Adam was once in the Garden of Eden.

One of my father's memories, and a story he used to tell us, was when visiting his wealthy relatives at their haciendas. Dad observed the landowners' behavior toward their servants. In the evenings, once the heat of the day was cooling down, these men would relax in their hammocks, visiting with people gathered around them. While laying on their hammocks a young servant boy would come with a bucket of clean water, a wash basin, and clean towel. The boy would untie the master's shoe, remove the sock, gently wash the foot, dry it, and put clean sandals on. Then the servant boy said, *"Lord, I am done washing your foot; please give me your other foot."* The master angrily replied, *"You lazy boy, you need to pick up your bucket and go around to my other side where my other foot is!"* The master would decry out loud spilling a slew of insults to his young servant, always expecting full submission. This practice of servitude is still

---

95. John 15:15

unfortunately a common practice, the master demanding complete and unquestionable subjugation.

Although sin ruptured the open relationship with our true Lord, Jesus came to restore us to the point of even washing his disciples' feet. Jesus became our Servant so that we can become His friend.

While enjoying our unique friendship with Jesus, on earth we still need true friends, which are difficult to find. Thanks to the prayer my friend Lynette taught me, I have been blessed throughout my life with true friends — not perfect friends but loving and supporting friends. To avoid the risk of omitting a dear and faithful friend, I will not name all of them, but just a few. One thing I know, since kindergarten sharing moments with Patricia, the wonderful childhood memories with Paquito and later Anita; my adventurous partner in Hamburg, Miriam; learning about Jesus with Elizabeth as a teenager; the giggly and studious friends from high school — Chichi and Patricia; the sweet Charito from the local church in Santa Cruz; my unique college classmates and friends from Montemorelos University — among them Lynette, my roommate Angie, and my study friend Ahmed; my dearest friend in Denver, Colorado, Angel, when I was a newlywed; the loving and supporting friends at Andrews University — Charo, Dan, Diane, Tei-Tei, Karen, Deby, and Ron; the supportive and patient friend in Bakersfield, Greg, who married James and me; the loyal and trustworthy coworkers like Joanne and Linda; and the list goes on, I feel immensely blessed.

Loving friends accept us just as we are, yet they encourage us to be better, opening up their souls for spiritual growth, they share their failures as well as triumphs, laugh and weep, and clean away resentment. The most beautiful example of friendship in Bible times is Jonathan and David. 1 Samuel 18:1 says, *"Jonathan became one in spirit with David, and he loved him as himself."* Other translations say, *"They became bound together;" "there was an immediate bond;" "the souls of Jonathan and David were knit together;" "the soul of Jonathan was knit with the soul of David."*

I am extremely thankful for my true friends, for they have enriched my spiritual journey. I am especially thankful for my loving and redeeming friend Jesus, because I am not His servant, He considers me His friend. I want to be bound together, to have my soul knitted with His.

# 17. Who are my Brothers and Sisters? — Lessons of Forgiveness

*"Happy birthday to you… cumpleaños feliz…"* Each November 9 it is the sweet wake-up call going back to childhood when dad would come next to my bed and sing to me with my siblings to wake me up. Then the stories from six of my senior siblings began, *"When you were born, I remember you were in the maternity ward in a room right across where Coqui was born 11 months ago…; when you were a little girl we played with you and Coqui as if you two were our dolls…; when you were a newborn you almost died, mom would sit on her bed, legs crossed, cry, and feed you drop-by-drop with a liquid dropper…"*

"Coincidentally with Kitty's birthday, a day like today, but in 1953, there was a coup by FSB and dad, for the first time, had to flee without us knowing his whereabouts for several days. Mom became an overnight heroine unintentionally. With six children in tow at 26 years of age, with coupons for milk, meat, flour, etc. that were reduced by the political opponents. We must not forget to prevent history from repeating itself, however cir-

*cular it may be. That day caught us all off guard since Mom and her six children were in La Guardia where Uncle Rafael lived, and we were spending a few vacation days with him. We got back home, the house was empty, and we had another feeling of emptiness in our stomach for not knowing where dad was."*

My older siblings, Pimpi, Lita, Pepe, Buby, Chacho, Chichin, and Coqui, were excellent role models, and most of the time as children were loving. For each I had a nickname, to the point that one time I had fourteen nicknames, and then came even more. Kitty, Kitticita, Picu, Piculivi, Madrecita, Marcianita, Achsosito, Absuito, Bs-Bs, Pezcuezo e'bota, Italia, Fideito, Filistriqui, Tierrita, Abisá, Chiqui, Chiquitita, Shimm, and Catorce-Apodos. It is true that while growing up I didn't like many of them, mainly it was the way the two youngest boys, Chacho and Chichin said them, but as I grew up I began feeling their affection. Dad also had a son, Bismarck, who expressed his tenderness when he visited us.

Pimpi is impeccable, extremely clean, and very organized, strict, and attentive to follow the rules. I admired her qualities and continue seeking her wisdom. Lita expressed motherly love. While in high school she took care of Coqui and me in the afternoons while mother worked. Lita is very studious and a perfectionist, she is incessant with her advice that I really appreciate. Then comes my beloved Pepe who would call me *Madrecita* (little mother), and *Marcianita* (little Martian). There was a popular song in the early 1960s about a *Marcianita* that Pepe would sing to me. Pepe has many qualities, but the biggest of them all is his warm love that penetrates the bones.

Buby was poetic and came up with the *Catorce-Apodos* (Fourteen-Nicknames) sonnet. He was very stoic and inherited the Teutonic discipline of our ancestors, yet he was also very loving. Chacho was a rascal, smart and mischievous, tricking Coqui and me every time he could. As adults, we worked together. During those four years I learned more than during my college education—I still seek him for professional advice. Quiet Chichin enjoyed making fun of the "little ones" (Coqui and me). Somehow he perceived that I didn't like being called the new nickname my dad had given me. Therefore, he would use every opportunity when dad wasn't watching to call me those 'ugly words' and make me cry. Yet Chichin is a Christ-loving adult, and lives to serve those in need. And my beloved Coqui, needless to say, my friend in Christ. From my brother Bismarck, I learned resilience and courage, his best attributes.

Growing up we had our differences, slowly we learned to respect our differences and learn from them, to admire one another and to support each other. We lost our brother Buby when he was only 57 years old, we had already lost dad, and years later we lost mom. Our losses strengthened our bond. Despite our religious beliefs, we pray to the same God and lift each other up in prayer.

In Matthew 12 and Luke 8, we read an episode of Jesus' life,

*"While Jesus was still talking to the crowd, his mother and brothers stood outside, wanting to speak to him. Someone told him, "Your mother and brothers are standing outside, wanting to speak to you." He replied to him, "Who is my mother, and who are my brothers?" Pointing to his disciples, he said, "Here are my mother and my brothers. For whoever does the will of my Father in heaven is my brother and sister and mother."* [96]

With all our failures, I am blessed with my brothers and sisters, they love God and share their love with those around them. I admire their attributes and want to keep learning from them. Yet the greatest lessons from my siblings developed during a seventeen-year period.

*"Kitty has died. To me, she doesn't exist,"* was the claim my brother Buby said to my beloved brother-in-law Adolfo Meave (Lita's) husband. It had been over ten years that Buby had decided not to talk to me and treat me with indifference, as if I did not exist. His resentment stemmed from a reaction I made while visiting my parents in Santa Cruz in 1989. His two youngest boys were playing outdoors sitting in a hammock and I felt they were bullying my little girl, Vanessa, who was around four years younger. My maternal and protective instincts made me react abruptly, and Buby could not forgive that I had been rude to his 'sweet and darling' little Alejandro, his 'most kind' and beloved child.

Hindsight is full of wisdom, yet when we live the mo-

---

96. Matthew 12:46-49

ment, it is only the power of the Holy Spirit that can refrain us from reactions that we will regret for the rest of our lives. *"Please forgive me,"* I pleaded to Buby to his response, *"Only God forgives, I am not God."* Thereafter my plea was to God, *"Oh Lord, please forgive, please heal our hearts, please bless Buby, please, please, please."*

The years of that regrettable incident in 1989 kept passing by and still no words from Buby. Even my brother-in-law Adolfo tried to reason with Buby as a friend and mature adults to no avail.

*"Kitty?"* was the voice on the other side of the phone line. *"Kitty, mom will be having her second knee-replacement surgery. You need to go to Santa Cruz and help us take care of mom. But don't worry, I will be there as well and will help you."* It was my sister Pimpi calling from Lima, Peru, while I was living in Southern California. Of the four daughters mom had—Pimpi, Lita, Coqui and Kitty, none of us lived in Santa Cruz, only the boys with their wives. They were loving and provided excellent company for my mom. When it came to more personal and constant care, like in a medical condition, the boys would call the girls to fly back home and help.

As the eldest sibling, Pimpi was the first one to be contacted and coordinate our schedules. Additionally, we all relied on Pimpi as she was an excellent nurse, and her husband was a physician. Pimpi's knowledge in the medical field has been admirable; therefore, she has been the go-to person for medical advice. Needless to say, Pimpi's nursing skills are still remembered as a loving, caring, and exceptional nurse.

*"Oh, Pimpi, I am glad you will be in Santa Cruz as well to take care of mom. I will certainly go and help you with mom's care."* My distress was because once mom became a widow, Buby had become very close to her. *"Oh, Lord, how can I do it?"* Yet I had the comfort that Pimpi was going to be on my side.

*"Kitty?"* was the voice on the other side of the phone line. *"Kitty, I will not be able to fly to Santa Cruz. You will have to take care of mom alone."* This was Pimpi's voice again. *"Oh no,"* was my silent response. *"How can I do it? How can I take care of mom and endure Buby's rejection all alone without Pimpi as a buffer? I will be alone, Lord, please help me,"* was my afflicted cry. As in years past, my Heavenly Father had a response:

> *"Marlene, Marlene, this is what the LORD says — he who created you, he who formed you, "Do not fear, for I have redeemed you; I have summoned you by name; you are mine. ² When you pass through the waters, I will be with you; and when you pass through the rivers, they will not sweep over you. When you walk through the fire, you will not be burned; the flames will not set you ablaze."* [97]

Filled with the confidence that the Lord was by my side, I flew to Santa Cruz to take care of mom and face the

---

97. Isaiah 43:1-2

customary painful dismissal. One afternoon, after mom's knee surgery, she and I were alone in her hospital room while she was recovering. Around 1:00 PM, Buby came to visit mom with his now grown son Alejandro. Buby went straight to her bed to talk to mom. There was no acknowledgement of my presence, he turned around and was ready to leave, then he looked at me and said, *"Do you want to join us for lunch?"* No other words were necessary, forgiveness had taken place, Buby allowed the work of the Holy Spirit to forgive me. I got up to follow Buby, looked back to see mom, we both smiled, and she winked at me.

After mom was discharged, Buby came one evening to visit her at home. Around 10:00 PM he got up to leave and gave me a loving embrace. I was traveling back home the next day. Buby uttered no words, his loving touch said it all. It was the last time we saw each other, a year later he died of pancreatic cancer.

The words of Jesus resonate in me, *"With man this is impossible, but not with God; all things are possible with God."*[98] Praise God for working in our impossible hearts. *"Here are my mother and my brothers. For whoever does the will of my Father in heaven is my brother and sister and mother."* How blessed I am for my loving brothers and sisters.

---

98. Mark 10:27

# 18. Beloved Nephews and Nieces

*"Let the little children come to me, and
do not hinder them, for the kingdom of
heaven belongs to such as these."* [99]

There was a knock at the door. We didn't move, it was too
cold to see who would be at our house at this late evening
hours on such a cold, windy winter night. Coqui and I were
cuddling in bed under a warm llama wool blanket, listening with our older sister Pimpi to a radio show. Suddenly,
Chichin opened our bedroom door holding a paper in his
shaking hands and repeating over and over again the tele-
gram message we had just received *"Nació varón el hijo de
Lita."* — *"A son was given birth by Lita."* The first grandchild,
nephew, and son was just born on June 16, 1971. This great
excitement continued as my parents received the news of
the birth of their 25th grandchild who was born on July
4, 1995 — 24 years later. In the meantime, the next generation of great-grandchildren had already begun in 1994.

Mom indulged the grandchildren with plenty of love.

---

99. Matthew 19:14

Whenever she could travel to assist with the birth of a new baby, or visit them on vacation, she would do it. When they came to visit and stayed with her for a few weeks, she would take them to church. Always cautious and considerate of the parents' wishes, she would provide for each child the special attention they needed. Mom never interfered in any of the couples relationships. She was respectful of their child-rearing decisions, until it came time to teach them about Jesus. Only one time that I can remember, was mom challenged not to take some grandchildren to church. Her response was emphatic. *"It is written,"* she said. *"Let the little children come to me, and do not hinder them, for the kingdom of heaven belongs to such as these."*[100] Never again was she questioned.

Jesus knew the importance of being attentive in the children's early years of life. He wanted children to begin trusting God at an early age and seeking Him at all times for protection, love, and encouragement. Children are needy and dependent, not knowing the challenges of life. Children's reactions are based on emotions rather than reason. Yet Jesus said, *"The kingdom of heaven belongs to such as these."* Even if children are neglected by their parents, if a child is led to the Lord, their self-image changes, their sense of security begins to root. Jesus also used children as examples of faith that we, as adults, need to emulate.

Why did Jesus say those words? *"The kingdom of heaven*

---

100. Idem

*belongs to such as these."* Let's think about it, children are innocent. Jesus loves anyone, young or old, *"red, or yellow, black, or white, all are precious in his sight,"* as long as we come to Him with a pure heart—the innocent heart of a child seeking His reassurance to be loved, accepted, and protected. Jesus knows that in this world we will be surrounded by wolves. He wants to embrace us, while sending his angels to shield us from this evil world.

It is important to remember that children in Jesus' time were not necessarily regarded as special or particularly endearing, except to their own parents. Many cultures today look on children as especially sweet, innocent, and even wise. Jewish culture in that day probably did not see children in such charming ways. The disciples most likely rebuked those bringing the children to Jesus because they felt it was socially improper, or because they thought the children would bother Jesus. It is likely that their move to hinder the parents from bringing their children to Jesus was motivated not by unkindness but by a desire to respect Jesus' position as a teacher. On the other hand, Jesus wanted the children to come to Him. He said, "Let the children come," because He wanted children learning to trust him at a young age, to love Him, and seek Him at all times, even when circumstances would hinder them to be near Jesus. Jesus longed to bless the children with the peace only He can impart, the confidence of knowing they have a truthful and perfect Father, the reassurance that He will never leave them nor forsake them. Jesus could only accomplish this deep yearning if the children came to Him. He is always ready to nurse us; we just need to come to Him—just as we are.

It is wonderful to think of Jesus interacting with a child. Scripture often compares believers to children.[101] In fact, Jesus told those following Him, *"Truly I tell you, unless you change and become like little children, you will never enter the kingdom of heaven. Therefore, whoever takes the lowly position of this child is the greatest in the kingdom of heaven."*[102] Jesus loved children's humility, dependance, and trust.

Jesus's command to *"let the little children come to me"* reveals several truths. First, children need to be blessed by the Lord. The Lord wants to bless the children. Parents should be encouraged to bring their children to Jesus at an early age and teach them His ways. Jesus has regard for the weakest and most vulnerable among us. No matter how compassionate Jesus's followers are, Jesus Himself is more compassionate still. And finally, those who come to Christ must do so in childlike humility, faith, and simplicity. Like children who implicitly trust their parents, we need to emulate their behavior of trusting Jesus and God. Faith is not about knowing everything or doing everything right. Faith is the certainty of knowing that no matter what happens, our Father in Heaven will take care of us. Depending on Him, even when life is terrifying and sad and makes no sense, is what makes a believer like a child. *"All those the*

101. Luke 10:21; Galatians 4:19; 1 John 4:4
102. Matthew 18:3–4; cf. Mark 10:15

*Father gives me will come to me, and whoever comes to me I will never drive away."*[103]

As my nephews grew older, my mother watched them with pride, and continuously prayed for their spiritual life. Once they began having their own children, it was time to love and pray for the new generation. I hold each of them dearly in my heart. My mom is no longer here to pray for them, but I can follow her legacy. As time, distance, and finances allowed, I tried attending important events in their lives — graduations, weddings, or birth of a new child. Every word I write in these memoirs is with the purpose of being a blessing to my beloved nephews and nieces. Each story has been prayed for over and over again. Even if only the life of one of my beloved nephews and nieces, or their own children, is blessed and changed by these stories, it was worth every minute of the long hours writing them.

My prayer is for their faith to be anchored in the Lord. The same Lord who was my mom's refuge and fortress in her times of troubles. The same Lord who is my Father, Husband, and Friend. To them I leave the great words found in the book *Education*.

> *"The greatest want of the world is the want of men and women — ladies and gentlemen who will not be bought or sold, who in their inmost souls are true and honest, who do not fear to call sin by its right name, whose conscience is as true to duty*

---

103. John 6:37

*as the needle to the pole, who will stand for the right though
the heavens fall.*[104]

This is my prayer for my beloved nephews and nieces,
and for their growing children.

---

104. E.G. White, Education, page 43. 1903, Copyright 2014 Ellen G. White
Estate, Inc.

# 19. Kill them with Love — My Greatest Teachers

*"A new command I give you: Love one another.*
*As I have loved you, so you must love one*
*another. By this everyone will know that you*
*are my disciples if you love one another."* [105]

*"I would like you to write a list of your greatest teachers,"* my dear executive coach Eileen used to say. *"Oh, Fraulein Klein, Frau Ludicke, Profita LeGrand, Dr. Jamison, Dr. Sanchez, Dr. Tucker, Dr. Jones, … ?"* I immediately thought. I had learned so much in kindergarten from the loving Fraulein Klein, she taught me to be creative. Frau Ludicke in Hamburg was not only a mathematics teacher and our class sponsor, but she also took notice of our individual needs. Once a week at 7:00 AM we met at the Kellinghussen Strasse swimming pool for one hour of swimming to increase our energy. She would take us on field trips, including one week at the island of Sylt in the North Sea with our bicycles in tow to

---

105. John 13:34, 35

get us out of our comfort zone. In college I learned wisdom from Profita LeGrand, an analytical mind from Dr. Jamison, and research skills from Dr. Sanchez. And in graduate school to have an inquisitive mind from Dr. Tucker, plus a very caring attitude from Dr. Jones.

However, Eileen wasn't referring to the wonderful teachers that had blessed my path. Eileen was referring to the most difficult people I had encountered and needed to have a continued relationship with them, generally at work. The homework had more to do with finding the strengths of the individuals with whom I felt intimidated by. These were the people who pulled a kryptonite on me and left me powerless.

Hmmm, it is not an easy task to reflect on those who hurt you. How can we appreciate the people we feel we have been harmed by? In Matthew 5:44, we read the words of Jesus, *"but I tell you, love your enemies and pray for those who persecute you,"* however, can we really love those who harm us? Eileen was right, it began by recognizing who those persons were, making a list of them, writing what caused the perceived challenge, and begin praying for them.

At some point in our lives, we all encounter difficult people, and feel rejection, yet we learn to deal with them and move on. The challenge becomes when despotism is constant to the point of affecting our health. It seems like being in an endless dream where you are trapped and feeling suffocated. *"Marlene, kill them with love,"* my great and patient boss Michael used to tell me. Love is a tool nobody can resist, true love disarms people, leaves them speechless, aghast, and impotent. As powerful as love is, so is hate. It was envy and covetousness that turned a shining angel, Lucifer, into our archenemy. It was hatred and jealousy that killed our Savior on the cross. Yet before and after the cross Jesus encouraged us to *"love your enemies and pray for those who persecute you."*

Why did an executive coach emphasize the need to recognize *'our greatest teachers?'* Why did Jesus encourage us to love our enemies and pray for those who persecute us? Our human nature is sociable, we were born with the need of belonging and acceptance. Thus, rejection affects our inner being. The ancient Greeks applied ostracism as a way to expel citizens from their community for ten years—it was the worst punishment an individual could receive. Babies and puppies have been subjected to multiple research projects by isolating them from social interaction with disastrous results.

Our Creator, *"who knit us together in our mother's womb, who created our inmost being,"*[106] knew our needs, gave his disciples the advice to precisely overcome these circumstances. John 14 through 17 is a box filled with gems.

How do we love our enemies? Jesus says it starts by praying for them. He knew that it is difficult to hate those we are praying for. His last week before being rejected, hated, and crucified, Jesus filled his disciples with advice.

---

106. Psalm 139: 13

First, Jesus gave his disciples hope. Jesus was going to his Father with the goal to prepare a place for us so that one day we could be with him again. When facing rejection, we should never give up hope. The circumstances are transitory, our God is eternal, ever and always present (omnipresent). When feeling that our gem box is empty, never give up hope.

Next Jesus promised his disciples an Advocate, the Holy Spirit. In court trials it is vital to have a good advocate. Even at work, a place where we spend more hours than at home during the week, we need to feel supported. The beauty of the Holy Spirit is that He is always and everywhere with us; He will even speak on our behalf, represent us, impress people's hearts, encourage us, and lift us up. Living with the image of the Holy Spirit at our side, there is no need to fear our greatest teachers. And finally, Jesus prayed to his Father for us. There are times when we stop praying—we don't have the energy, the courage, or the faith to pray any longer. But Jesus, the Holy Spirit and the holy angels never give up on us. When the storm is over and we reflect back, we realize that we were never alone.

*"Marlene, kill them with love,"* I can still hear the voice of my great boss. Slowly the bullies left the company with their own self-inflicted shame. Slowly their followers spoke to me and recognized their actions, many times apologizing. In the meantime, I remembered John 14 to 17 and the words in of the prophet Micah:

*"And what does the Lord require of you? To act justly and to love mercy, and to walk humbly with your God."[107]*

After all, maybe I am someone else's greatest teacher. I do hope though, that I am a great teacher because of positive influence. Therefore, I would always need to reexamine my heart, my motives, my actions, and reactions. Then I asked myself the questions: *"Am I being just? Am I displaying mercy? Am I walking humbly with my God? What is the image people are seeing of Marlene?—Just another teacher or a loving coworker?* Now I need to remember to always *"love my 'enemies' and constantly pray for those who persecute me."*

---

107. Micah 6:8

# 20. Amazing Grace

*"Amazing grace! How sweet the sound, that
saved a wretch like me! I once was lost but
now am found, was blind but now I see."[108]*

Growing up, especially if we are raised reading Bible stories of miracles and marveling about God's amazing grace,
we also want to be witnesses of His miracles and grace. *"Oh
Lord, show me your glory,"[109]* asked Moses to the Lord. And
what did God show Moses? His grace. *"Then the Lord came
down in the cloud and stood there with him and proclaimed his
name, ..., "The Lord, the Lord, the compassionate and gracious God, slow to anger, abounding in love and faithfulness,
maintaining love to thousands, and forgiving wickedness, rebellion and sin."[110]* The Lord also showed Moses His grace
in many wonders like opening the Red Sea and saving and
the whole nation from being slaughtered by the sword of
Pharaoh and his troops.

*"Oh, Lord, show me your grace; and please help me to be*

---

108. John Newton
109. Exodus 33:18
110. Exodus 34: 6,7

*gracious,"* were many of my prayers. Little did I realize that I was witnessing His true grace with the loving and patient man called my husband, James.

*"What do you need or expect from a relationship?"* Was one of my first questions when James and I met on www.adventistsingles.com in September 2010. *"Patience,"* was his response. Hmmm, I wondered why. As an introvert, he slowly shared his challenges, and I could observe his need for a patient friend, companion, and spouse. He was and still is a very thoughtful person and takes time to act as he analyzes all options before making a final decision. This time though, he was impatient while praying for a special friend, Kathy, that used to be his wife. Kathy had moved to another nation with Jay, a person she met online. *"Oh, dear Lord, I plea to you for Kathy's salvation,"* were James's constant prayers, day after day, week after week. He visited Kathy's parents, they all shared tears and prayed for Kathy.

*"James,"* was the sweet voice he heard one sunny Sabbath afternoon while meditating on his couch, *"if you want Kathy to be saved, you need to forgive Jay."* The new journey of forgiveness began, by the grace of a loving heavenly Father, James was able to forgive Jay and Kathy and reconcile a friendship that had lasted 27 years. Thanks to James's forgiveness, Kathy's family became part of our extended family.

Yet our actions are not isolated, they carry consequences unbeknownst to us. A young teen was witnessing and suffering turmoil as his mom Kathy moved away. James's and

Kathy's only son felt neglected, abandoned, left to make sense of this cruel world. He found company with other adolescents going through similar struggles. Their outlet was not faith, prayer, Bible study, and God. They were able to numb their pain with narcotics. Through the long ordeal was a loving and gracious father tending for his beloved son, day after day, night after night, week after week. He ensured he was fed, he helped him bathe and get dressed. He took his beloved son everywhere with him as long as he could. He showered him with love and embraced him while saying, *"Matthew, Jesus loves you; I love you, and I am glad you are here."* Yet this world was too painful for the son and one morning he never woke up from his sleep. In his mercy, God had given him rest and peace.

*"You will see him again,"* were the words from the local church pastor, *"your son will be saved, because of your faith the Lord will honor His promise that Christ came to seek and save the lost."*[111]. Matthew's life was cut short, too soon, too painful for a loving dad. Yet our Lord and Savior will complete His work to perfection when He returns to redeem each of us. On earth, our stories will always remain unfinished. When we get to heaven, they will be culminated with Jesus welcoming us into His Kingdom.

As I observe James's grace and faith, I feel special to share my life with a person with so much grace. His forgiveness to Kathy and Matthew makes me understand

---

111. Luke 19:10

better how marvelous that we rely on a God, our Lord, who is gracious with us to the end, always merciful, long-suffering, and full of longanimity. After all, my prayers for miracles experiencing God's grace were being answered in an unusual and subtle way. James's life explains the words of Harry Ironside, "Grace is the very opposite of merit... Grace is not only undeserved favor, but it is favor, shown to the one who has deserved the very opposite."

*"By grace we have been saved through faith. And this is not our own doing; it is the gift of God."*[112] Praise God for His grace and His gift that we can also be graceful (loving, merciful, and forgiving) to those around us. And because of God's amazing grace, we wretched will see our beloved ones again. My dear James will be able to embrace his beloved Matthew and have him around forever.

---

112. Ephesians 2:8

# 21. A Continuous Journey — My Sweet Valerie

*"I have told you these things, so that in me you may*
*have peace. In this world you will have trouble.*
*But take heart! I have overcome the world."*[113]

*"Do you know when are they going to transfer me to my room?"*
asked my daughter Valerie after spending a whole night
in the Emergency Room (ER) at Vanderbilt University
Medical Center in Nashville, Tennessee, on Sunday,
October 30, 2021. For the last ten months, we had been
running from ER rooms in Chattanooga, Tennessee, from
Erlanger's main hospital to Erlanger's East needing treatment for Valerie's advanced medical condition. *You need to
go to Vanderbilt,"* a medical friend recommended. So, there
we were, 24 hours later still waiting to be transferred to a
room. All ER beds are busy; therefore, Valerie was given a
bed in a hallway close to the ambulance entrance and I was
blessed to find a chair where I could raise my legs.

---

113. John 16:13

The night was busy, we could hear and feel all the commotion of a busy Saturday night. A kind nurse kept watch over Valerie, he was able to stabilize her. *"Can there be any more interruptions, and noise, and cold air in this hallway?" "What time is it anyway? Oh, 6:30 AM, better make an effort to stay awake. And what are all the voices at the end of the hallway? Oh, it is a shift change."* I turned around and saw the excitement of the incoming nurse crew, all huddled and beginning their Halloween parade before their shift began.

Dressed with courage, I got up and looked for something to eat. After a cup of spiced tea with a bagel, I realized my longing was for peace, spending time with my Lord, listening to His voice. *"Marlene, Marlene,"* He said, *"Remember? In this world you will have trouble. But take heart! I have overcome the world."*[114]

This is what I call 'Perfect Peace.' It doesn't matter what our circumstances are, with whom we are, or where we are. If we can experience the presence of the Lord and we are able to hear His voice, this is what brings perfect peace to our souls. It is Jesus's presence, companionship, compassionate heart, and healing hands that we need. And this perfect peace nobody can take away. I am reminded of the words of King David, *"Great peace have those who love your law, and nothing can make them stumble."*[115]

In other words, Christmas Day, December 25, 2021 arrived. Valerie was discharged from Vanderbilt just a couple

114. John 16: 33
115. Psalm 119:165

of days before Thanksgiving. Since then, Valerie had been hospitalized twice. Actually, on Christmas Day, December 25, 2021, she was at Erlanger East. James and I visited her to spend a few hours on Christmas Eve. She was admirable. Although in pain, she seemed to be peace. A kind nurse before leaving her shift at 7:00 PM came and gave Valerie a book about prayer she had authored. Susie Jones dedicated the book to Valerie with the words *"hope to see you in heaven."* Susie assured Valerie that she will be praying for her.

How do you understand sickness and pain? When Jesus was on earth, He performed multiple miracles healing the sick and raising the dead. Although many villages were temporarily not experiencing illness because of Jesus's presence in their midst, some other villages were not as blessed. Why not? It is not for us to question the Lord; our role is to understand His purpose.

The subject of suffering requires multiple volumes to analyze. It is a mystery too deep to unravel because it began in a perfect and harmonious heaven. Although we could consider the Bible as a book of the battles between good and evil, in the end, good prevails. Jesus won the battle on the cross, and because of His victory, we can also experience it when He returns and takes us back with Him to heaven. He promised us *"I am going away, and I am preparing a place for you, and I will come back and take you to be with me that you also may be where I am."*[116]

---

116. John 14:3

Isn't this a wonderful promise? Jesus is not telling me, *"I will heal Valerie."* He is saying, *"I am preparing a place for Valerie and all your family where you will be with me!"* Isn't this a better promise than just a temporary healing touch?

It was a Christmas Eve when I was a little girl of probably five years old, and I was hospitalized in Santa Cruz. I don't recall the reason, but I remember being in my room alone because mom had to be home taking care of the whole family and preparing for the large traditional Christmas Eve meal. Before the evening arrived, dad came to my room and told me that he was taking me home (he probably had already cleared my discharge procedure with the medical and nursing staff). All I remember is that dad picked me up and took me in his arms all the way home; we walked the solitary roads, and I was in dad's arms. We got home with enough time for me to take a bath, change my clothes to festive garments, and enjoy the delicious meal mom had prepared for all of us.

Christ will come back. His angels are going to pick up each one of us, reunite us with our loved ones, and give us a new garment so that we can join Jesus with our clean new garments at the feast He has prepared for us in the presence of His Father. What else can we ask? This is what I call perfect joy and a perfect Merry Christmas.

Once again, I remember my heavenly Father's loving voice, *"I have told you these things, so that in me you may have peace. In this world you will have trouble. But take heart! I have overcome the world.*"[117] Jesus promised, *⁴"They will walk with me, dressed in white, for they are worthy.⁵ The one who is victorious will, like them, be dressed in white. I will never blot out the name of that person from the book of life but will acknowledge that name before my Father and his angels."*[118] Jesus will give us his white garment to join Him and His Father to dine with Him at the banquet He has prepared for us. Oh, what a day of joy that will be!

Jesus's promises fill me with joy and peace. I will meditate in them until our savior returns.

> *"I am coming soon. Hold on to what you have, so that no one will take your crown. ¹² The one who is victorious I will make a pillar in the temple of my God. Never again will they leave it. I will write on them the name of my God and the name of the city of my God, the new Jerusalem, which is coming down out of heaven from my God; and I will also write on them my new name."*[119]

A New Heaven and a New Earth

> *"¹Then I saw "a new heaven and a new earth," for the first heaven and the first earth had passed away, and there was no longer any sea. ² I saw the Holy City, the new Jerusalem, coming down out of heaven from God, prepared as a bride*

---

117. John 16:13
118. Revelation 3:4-5
119. Revelation 3: 11-12

*beautifully dressed for her husband. [3] And I heard a loud voice from the throne saying, "Look! God's dwelling place is now among the people, and he will dwell with them. They will be his people, and God himself will be with them and be their God. [4] 'He will wipe every tear from their eyes. There will be no more death'[b] or mourning or crying or pain, for the old order of things has passed away. [5] He who was seated on the throne said, "I am making everything new!" Then he said, "Write this down, for these words are trustworthy and true. [6] He said to me: "It is done. I am the Alpha and the Omega, the Beginning, and the End. To the thirsty I will give water without cost from the spring of the water of life. [7] Those who are victorious will inherit all this, and I will be their God and they will be my children."[120]*

---

120. Revelation 21:1-7

# Epilogue

*"May my heart be broken by what*
*breaks the heart of Jesus."* [121]

The year 2022 came and went as with the blink of an eye. Friday, December 30, 2022 arrived with the normal expectations of the New Year and 2023, a year of life, health, and happiness. Yet we had to learn another lesson of love, patience, and resilience. At midnight on December 30, Valerie needed to be intubated for sepsis. We don't know what caused it, all I remember is watching her limb and stiff body in my arms four times and my extreme agony observing her pain and what I thought was the loss of her young and fragile life. After being intubated, Valerie was in an induced coma in ICU, and at the third day she tolerated the extubation. Her dad, Hugo, and sister Vanessa had come to spend Christmas with us. On Friday, Vanessa had returned to her home back in Apex, North Carolina. I praised the Lord that Hugo was with us all the time. Vanessa flew back to be with her sister. Valerie's recovery was

---

121. Bob Pierce. Founder of World Vision

incredible, on Tuesday, January 3, the medical personnel expressed their astonishment, stating that her recuperation exceeded their expectations. Valerie responded, *"My whole family was praying for me."* Indeed, her family and extended family of friends and churches all around the world. During my morning meditations I heard the words of the Lord, *"Forget the former things; do not dwell on the past. See, I am doing a new thing!"*[122] Yes, the Lord has a plan for us, He will make everything new and that is all I need to trust and put my hope on.

The words of the Apostle Paul resonate in my mind, *"Being confident of this, that He who began a good work in you will carry it on to completion until the day of Christ Jesus,"*[123] What a blessed promise!

These memoires are part of my spiritual odyssey. They allowed me to reflect on the eternal while journeying through a transient life. All along I prayed for guidance and wisdom, to leave messages of hope and assurance that we are not alone — although at times we may feel like it. Jesus promised his disciples the outpouring of the Holy Spirit as their Companion, Comforter, and Protector. Through biblical history we read how the Lord sent His host of angels to fight human battles. Jesus pledged our salvation through His own blood. Why then should we live in fear and be discouraged?

Children and even adults get entertained and hopeful to

---

122. Isaiah 43: 18, 19
123. Philippians 1:6

obtain the powers of fictional characters, to no avail. They search for an illusion and get discouraged when they don't find it. *"How can I find strength, dear Father in Heaven? How can I endure another trial? How can I reflect Jesus? How do I obtain your wisdom? How, how, how?"* are my constant prayers. Once again His sweet and peaceful voice comes, *"Marlene, Marlene, I pray that the eyes of your heart may be enlightened in order that you may know the hope to which he has called you, the riches of his glorious inheritance in his holy people, [19] and his incomparably great power for us who believe. That power is the same as the mighty strength [20] he exerted when he raised Christ from the dead."[124]*

*"Oh, the power that raised Jesus from death is available for me?"* — *"Yes, that is exactly what I mean. Can you think of any greater power?"* *"Wow, incroyable,"* are my thoughts. Have you ever imagined the power Jesus had to heal and break the chains of a demon-possessed man? Have you pondered in the exceeding outburst of energy to raise himself from the dead? The release of energy that raised Jesus from the dead caused an earthquake in all the known world to the point that even other dead saints were raised from their tombs. That same power is available to us, to you and me, that abundant loving energy is promised to us to transform us to the original image created in the Garden of Eden, until *"He who began a good work in you will carry it on to completion."*

---

124. Ephesian 1:18-20

*"Oh, dear Lord, help me to never forget how difficult life is without Jesus,"* is my prayer.

What else can we ask when we truly understand the Lord's voice, *"For I know the plans I have for you,"* declares the LORD, *"plans to prosper you and not to harm you, plans to give you hope and a future?"*[125] Oh, this verse overflows my heart with joy, the Lord wants to prosper me. It fills my mind with peace, He will not harm me. He will bring me hope and a future. As I look back, He already executed His promise.

Yet in our journey we do get tired and discouraged, once again my devoted friend says, *"But those who hope in the LORD will renew their strength. They will soar on wings like eagles; they will run and not grow weary; they will walk and not be faint."*[126]

There are times when I wonder if my belief in God, my caring Father, beloved Friend, and Faithful Husband is true. There are so many philosophies and debates about the true God, His existence, and all the attributes we assign to Him. My early experiences in life were of controversies and disagreements about the personal expression of our faith. In my adult life, these arguments among people have not changed. Maybe someone may assert that I am wrong, and that I do not know. One thing I am certain of is that only eternity will tell. Yet during this transient life, I had joy, I had peace, I felt and experienced the loving touch of my

125. Jeremiah 29:11
126. Isaiah 40:31

amazing God, His Faithful Son, and Comforting Spirit. If Martin Luther was able to begin a worldwide reformation that has endured through centuries, then I can also learn from the same source Martin Luther had and become an agent of change. He had the Bible, and so do I. The only difference is how much time we spend reading it and meditating on it.

May each of the readers seek the same Savior that loved me to the point of giving His life for me. I will continue to pray for it and live a life that my epitaph would read, *"Marlene, a woman who loved God with all her heart."*

My deepest desire for my readers is that each of you gets to *"See God more clearly, to love Him more dearly, and to follow Him more nearly."*[127] To experience an amazing journey to inner joy and peace. Remembering that accepting Jesus is a single experience, getting to know Jesus as our most beloved and faithful Friend is a journey of a lifetime.

---

127. Hymn attributed to Richard of Chichester

# About the Author

She's talented and has unique abilities, loves family, traveling, reading, and most of all writing. When she was seven years old her father spent his evenings at the dinner table typing his first book. Sitting next to her dad Marlene began a manuscript, *The Adventures of Kitty Kreidler*, (her family nickname). As she grew, she loved reading and writing poetry, later she began journaling her spiritual walk. At college, she researched and wrote excellent essays. At work, she used her skills in writing handbooks and business plans. When a good friend invited her to a writing club, she decided to be serious and compile her spiritual epiphanies. Her dream during retirement is to travel and write.

With German and French grandparents Marlene was born in Santa Cruz, Bolivia, and is the youngest of eight children. Her siblings, nephews, and nieces live all around the world which makes traveling a double joy. She has a master's degree in leadership from Andrews University. Her oldest daughter Vanessa lives in North Carolina. Marlene, her husband James McKamey, and her daughter Valerie live in Ooltewah, Tennessee.

CPSIA information can be obtained
at www.ICGtesting.com
Printed in the USA
BVHW041515020523
663428BV00004B/446